DEVELOPMENT AND UNDERDEVELOPMENT
Series editors: Ray Bromley and Gavin Kitching

*Development and the
Environmental Crisis*

RED OR GREEN ALTERNATIVES?

KT-165-398

In the same series

Development and the Environmental Crisis

RED OR GREEN ALTERNATIVES?

Michael Redclift

LONDON and NEW YORK

First published in 1984 by Methuen & Co. Ltd
Reprinted 1987
Reprinted by Routledge 1991
11 New Fetter Lane, London EC4P 4EE

Simultaneously published in the USA and Canada
by Routledge
a division of Routledge, Chapman and Hall, Inc.
29 West 35th Street, New York, NY 10001

© *1984 Michael Redclift*

Typeset by Scarborough Typesetting Services
Printed and bound in Great Britain by
Richard Clay Ltd, Bungay, Suffolk

All rights reserved. No part of this book may be reprinted or
reproduced or utilized in any form or by any electronic, mechanical or
other means, now known or hereafter invented, including photocopying and
recording, or in any information storage or retrieval system, without
permission in writing from the publishers.

British Library Cataloguing in Publication Data

   Redclift, Michael
     Development and the environmental crisis. —
     (Development and underdevelopment)
     1. Environmental policy.   2. World politics—
     1975–1985
     I. Title   II. Series
     333.7'2   HC79.E5

ISBN 0-415-06602-6 (pbk)

Library of Congress Cataloging in Publication Data

has been applied for

LANCASTER UNIVERSITY
17 OCT 1994
LIBRARY

94   01902

Contents

Series editors' preface

Development studies is a complex and diverse field of academic research and policy analysis. Concerned with the development process in all the comparatively poor nations of the world, it covers an enormous geographical area and a large part of the modern history of the world. Such a large subject area has generated a varied body of literature in a growing number of journals and other specialist publications, encompassing such diverse issues as the nature and feasibility of industrialization, the problem of small-scale agriculture and rural development in the Third World, the trade and other links between developed and developing countries and their effects on the development prospects of the poor, the nature and causes of poverty and inequality, and the record and future prospects of 'development planning' as a method of accelerating development. The nature of the subject matter has forced both scholars and practitioners to transcend the boundaries of their own disciplines whether these be social sciences, like economics, human geography or sociology, or applied sciences such as agronomy, plant biology or civil engineering. It is now a conventional wisdom of development studies that development problems are so multi-faceted and complex that *no* single discipline can hope to encompass them, let alone offer solutions.

This large and interdisciplinary area and the complex and rapidly changing literature pose particular problems for students, practitioners and specialists seeking a simple introduction to the field or some part of the field with which they are unfamiliar. The Development and Underdevelopment series attempts to rectify these problems by providing a number of brief, readable introductions to important issues in development studies written by an international range of specialists. All the texts are designed to be readily comprehensible to students meeting the issues for the first time, as well as to practitioners in developing countries, international agencies and voluntary bodies. We hope that, taken together, these books will bring to the reader a sense of the main preoccupations and problems in this rich and stimulating field of study and practice.

RAY BROMLEY
GAVIN KITCHING

Acknowledgements

This book would not have been written without the encouragement and support of a number of people. My colleagues in the Department of Environmental Studies at Wye College provided enthusiasm and support for the project. Gavin Kitching gave helpful advice and concrete suggestions at various points. My wife, Nanneke, discussed with me most of the points raised in the book and contributed generously to its argument. Paul Webster read the final version and helped to clarify a number of questions. Finally, Sheila Kingsnorth took time out from being a Super-Secretary to type the manuscript with efficiency and care.

Needless to say, none of the above is responsible for the opinions expressed in the book.

For my grandfather,
Marxist and Environmentalist

Earth, give me back your pure gifts,
the towers of silence which rose
from the solemnity of their roots.
I want to go back to being what I have not been,
and learn to return from such depths
that amongst all natural things
I could live or not live; it does not matter
to be one stone more, the dark stone,
the pure stone which the river bears away.

Pablo Neruda, *Memorial de Isla Negra* (1964)

Introduction

The 1960s and 1970s saw the growth of a critical literature in development studies, which took issue with neoclassical economics and gave rise to a substantial body of Marxist work on development. During the same period increasing international attention was paid to the growing threat to the environment in the developing countries. In the decade since the Stockholm Conference of 1972, which helped to launch the United Nations Environment Programme, this environmental threat has increased. The environmental crisis in the South is looked upon as a policy problem or, in popular imagination, it is seen as an Act of God. In neither case is it seen as a *political* issue, in the sense that a political response is necessary to avert the crisis, and that such a response would, inevitably, favour some interests over others in the global economy. The environment has not, in fact, been interpreted within the framework of global economic relations. It has not been part of the political dialogue about development and the analysis of underdevelopment.

There are several reasons for this omission. Any action which calls for international agreement is likely to meet with the objection of sovereign states and their governments. Also, attitudes towards the environment, and man's attitude towards nature generally, are curiously ambivalent. An explicitly political stance on the environment was slow to develop, even in those countries, like the United States, where the environmental movement had long roots. Much more notable, however, has been the tendency to characterize environmental conflict in the South as anything but *environmental*. Urban squatters were protesting about their social and economic 'marginality' rather than making environmental politics. Peasant movements were largely concerned with responding to political repression, rather than making essentially *environmental* demands. The tendency has existed for some time to depoliticize environmental issues at the international level, while considering resource conflict at the local or national level as other than environmental.

There are, in addition, reasons why political economy has failed to engage with the debate about the environment. Natural resources were never at the centre of the stage in Marxist thinking. Also, the environment was rarely looked upon as a distributive issue. It was a 'given' in the development situation of most countries, over which they had little control. Rather like the climate, natural resources were distributed according to rules that man did not invent, thus disputes between men about them were not inherently environmental. These disputes between men had their origin in the international economy and the class structure of individual countries.

This book is dedicated to demythologizing the 'environment' and questioning the facility with which the environment has been depoliticized. So many causes of the environmental crisis are structural, with roots in social institutions and economic relationships, that anything other than a political treatment of the environment lacks credibility. Thus, one objective of this book is to examine the distributive effects of the environmental crisis, in terms that are familiar to the 'political economy' tradition. Another is to discuss the position of those who *do* locate resource issues centre-stage – the environmentalists – in the light of a political economy analysis. The aim is to make the environmental crisis a central concern of political economy and its structural causes a central concern of environmentalism.

The argument of the book is that the resource crisis in the South is also a development crisis. It is suggested that both the development strategies based on the experience and interests of western capitalist countries, and those based on an alternative Marxist perspective, are seriously inadequate. Neither type of strategy is capable of generating better livelihoods for poor people from existing resources, without taking an unacceptable toll of the environment. As we shall see it is the poor who are the losers in the process of environmental depredation – whether this process is initiated by large-scale capital or whether they themselves act as the agents of resource depletion. In addition, the deficiencies of the development strategies being enacted in the South cannot simply be rectified by employing 'conservation' practices developed in the North. Conservation has a role to play in development, but the structural binds that link the developing countries to industrial society are such that tinkering with the environment cannot reverse long-term trends. If, as claimed in this book, environmental breakdown proceeds *because* of 'development', then applying 'conservation' management techniques to the South is often futile and unworkable.

The two closely related objectives of theoretical exposition and empirical documentation, which form the core of this book, are explored in succeeding chapters. At some points the concentration on theory takes the discussion away from the 'real world'. At others, the presentation becomes so engaged in the very tangible environmental problems of the real world that the theoretical issues might seem distant. It is hoped that, as the argument unfolds, both themes become interwoven in the material presented and in the mind of the reader.

The book is organized in the following way. The first chapter (Political economy and the environment) discusses the way in which a concern with the natural world became divorced from nineteenth-century political economy, including Marxism. It also draws attention to the way in which contemporary development theory, influenced by a political economy perspective, has neglected or minimized environmental factors. Chapter 2 (Global resource problems) sets out the context in which these perspectives have been developed by documenting the nature and scale of the global resource crisis and drawing attention to its class character. It argues that the way the resource crisis is discussed seriously *misrepresents* its distributive consequences, as well as its causes.

The ideological significance of 'environmentalism' is analysed at more length in Chapter 3 (Environmentalism and development), which questions the appropriateness of the environmental approaches derived from developed countries' experience for the less developed world. Beginning with a review of some of the key elements in an environmentalist perspective, the chapter goes on to discuss the political and ideological obstacles to implementing a more resource-conscious development strategy in the South. In the final section of this chapter the view proclaimed in the Brandt Reports, that North and South have a mutual interest in resolving their common crisis, is compared with the attempts of Rudolf Bahro to link the South's environmental crisis with northern rearmament and economic recession.

The following two chapters consider the juxtaposition of rural poverty and resource depletion in the South in more detail. Chapter 4 (Rural poverty and the environment) asks whether rural poverty is structurally induced, that is, attributable to economic relationships in the wider society, or largely attributable to the quality of the resource endowments on which the poor depend. Chapter 5 (Environmental conflict and development policy in rural Mexico) elaborates on this discussion by focusing on one country, Mexico, and examining the inter-relationship of the natural environment, and the structural processes represented by the growth of capitalist agriculture and state policy towards the rural poor. It concludes that both the relative and absolute socio-economic position of different groups is influenced by a combination of factors, both situational and structural. The key to a better understanding of environmental poverty lies in establishing the specific ways in which structural processes alter resource endowments.

Chapter 6 (Technology and the control of resources) examines the effects of technological change on the environment, and the benefits which different social classes derive from these changes. After discussing the implications of 'advanced' technologies for the less developed countries, the chapter considers whether, as has recently been claimed, the adoption of 'appropriate' technologies serves to reinforce the poverty of poor countries. The argument put forward is that, in line with the discussion in Chapter 2, some resources are currently acquiring a value which they did not previously possess, especially through developments in biotechnology research. Brazil's ethanol programme is reviewed for evidence of the social consequences of technological choice in areas such as biotechnology.

In the final chapter (Development and the environment: a converging discourse?) the argument developed throughout the book, that environmentalism and political economy would each benefit from cross-fertilization, is related to several themes in contemporary radical discourse. The 'bonding' of feminism, ecology and Marxism is examined in the light of current attempts to provide an alternative vision to that represented by patriarchal, industrial society. The implications of these approaches for the discourse on political economy and the environment are discussed and a new direction is tentatively advanced for future research and enquiry.

1

Political economy and the environment

The term 'political economy' has a long history. During the eighteenth and early nineteenth centuries what we refer to today as 'economics' was inseparable from the other social science disciplines such as politics, sociology and history. The early 'political economists' wrote within a broadly humanistic tradition and their interest in trade and manufacturing was partly motivated by the philosophical search for ways of maximizing human happiness. Adam Smith was aware that economic growth affected the position and role of the landed classes. John Stuart Mill considered that economic conditions were bound up with a complex web of 'institutions and social relations' (Mill 1873). In Marx's view, nineteenth-century economists were blinded by their belief in capitalism, but the degeneration of economics to which he referred was at that time in its infancy. The notion that economics, a product of capitalist society and thought, could be both an instrument of capitalist analysis and an 'objective' or 'neutral' science is largely a product of twentieth-century positivism.

'Political economy' is used here to refer to an approach to development which is derived principally from Marx, although the compass was shared by other contemporary political economists. This approach locates economic analysis within specific social formations, and explains development processes in terms of the benefits and costs they carry for different social classes. Policies for the amelioration of poverty, for example, or the protection of the environment, are regarded as the outcome of a struggle between class interests, negotiated by, and with, the state. We arrive at greater understanding of these policies not through recourse to dogma or empiricism, but by looking for 'the general in the particular and the particular in the general' (de Silva 1982: 7). Political economy recognizes the historical specificity of social formations, but seeks to explain structural variation within a coherent interpretative framework.

The argument developed below is that there is considerable common ground between historical materialism and a concern with the environment, but the emphasis in early political economy on the liberating aspects of economic growth forced a separation between 'development theory', in both its neoclassical and Marxist versions, and 'environmentalism'. One effect of this is that the 'political economy' perspective on development has failed to incorporate the environmentalist concern with sustainability. For too long social scientists have ignored the environment in the construction of development theory, while those interested in environmentalism have scarcely addressed the theoretical problems which their commitment raises.

In Marxist thought the major contradiction lay between the 'forces of production' (or substructure) and the 'relations of production' (superstructure). As Marx expressed it in his *Preface to a Contribution to the Critique of Political Economy*:

> In the social production of their life, men enter into definite relations that are indispensable and independent of their will, relations of production which correspond to a definite stage of development of their material productive forces. . . . At a certain stage of their development the material productive forces of society come into conflict with the existing relations of production.   (Marx and Engels 1970: 7)

What could not have been predicted in the lifetime of Marx or Engels was that capitalism would pose such a threat to natural resources that the very existence of development would be called into question. Furthermore, from the standpoint of our own times the political, legal and social fabric of society, the superstructure, is not merely an obstacle to the full realization of productive forces, it has also produced an environmentalist ideology which poses problems of credibility and legitimacy for the economic development model. Social movements arise, such as the Green Movement on the European continent, which seek to reverse the trends in capitalist development. They do so, moreover, at a time when the deepening economic crisis in the developed countries is being linked with the continuing underdevelopment of the South (Brandt 1980). A consciousness of the 'limits to growth', even in the developed countries, is married to a fear of imminent nuclear annihilation. The demise of the economic system lies in its profligate misuse of natural resources and its heavy dependence on the production and sale of nuclear armaments. Without the hindsight which history affords us it was impossible for the early Marxists to appreciate the full implications of the environmental crisis for political economy. We, who have inherited their mantle, should ensure that we take environmental problems seriously. As Aidan Foster-Carter wrote over a decade ago:

> Those who insist that such a process (environmental destruction) has nothing to do with Marxism merely ensure that what they choose to call Marxism will have nothing to do with what happens in the world.
>
> (Foster-Carter 1974: 94)

THE ENVIRONMENT IN MARXIST THOUGHT

For Marx, industrialization was a progressive force which harnessed technology to natural resources and permitted a reduced dependence on agriculture. In the third volume of *Capital* he wrote:

> One of the major results of the capitalist mode of production is that . . . it transforms agriculture from a mere empirical and mechanical self-perpetuating process employed by the least developed part of society, into the conscious scientific application of agronomy.
>
> (Marx 1974: 617)

The environment, particularly the rural environment, was transformed through the application of capital. Historically, those who owned the land had appropriated the value of the labour employed upon it through absolute ground rent. In nineteenth-century England, at least, a class of landlords continued to play an important role in appropriating surplus value not, as in the industrial sector, through re-creating capital, but through their ownership of a limited resource: land. Ground rent was surplus value, the product of surplus labour (ibid.: 634). Nevertheless, improved technology in agriculture and the stimulus to production provided by the growth of the non-agricultural population, ensured that 'constant capital' displaced 'variable capital' (Labour) in the production process. Under commodity production the ownership of land and its economic exploitation were separated; a class of farmers emerged who were dependent on differential rent derived from more efficient production on improved soil.

Capitalism developed, according to Marx, through the more efficient production and appropriation of surplus value, which implied new land and resource uses. The environment performed an enabling function, but all value was derived from the exploitation of labour power. It was impossible to conceive of a 'natural' limit to the material productive forces of society. The barriers that existed to the full realization of resource potential were imposed by property relations and legal obligations rather than than resource endowments. No contradiction existed between man's mastery of nature and his ability to exploit science for his own ends. From an historical materialist perspective it was society, not science, which placed restrictions on human potential.

Lenin elaborated on this view in his discussion of the relationship between man and nature. Man was a product of nature, but also a part of nature: 'Matter is primary, and thought, consciousness, sensation are products of a very high development. Such is the materialist theory of knowledge, to which natural science instinctively subscribes' (Lenin 1952: 69). The affinity between natural science, as it developed, and historical materialism was, in Lenin's view, undeniable. In fact *only* materialism was compatible with natural science. He noted that Engels had constantly referred to the 'laws of nature' or the 'necessities of nature' without considering it necessary to explain the generally known propositions of materialism (Lenin 1952: 156). Nature, like history, was subject to the dialectical laws of motion (259). Engels had observed this similarity and Lenin confirmed his support for 'the unity of mind and matter' which had played such an important role in both Marx's and Engels' thinking. As we shall see later in this chapter, the writing of other Marxists, notably Lenin and Rosa Luxemburg, elaborated on the relationship between Man and Nature in areas of colonial expansion. Their view remained, however, that capital could only fully appropriate surplus value through the conversion of nature to its own purposes.

Before considering these ideas in more detail it is worth reflecting on Engels' contribution to this debate. In two rather neglected essays written in 1875 and 1876, Engels puts forward a more contemporary-sounding version of the relationship between man and his environment. First, in his 'Introduction to the Dialectics of Nature', Engels asserts that man had shaped nature from his beginnings (Engels 1970a: 66). After the publication of Darwin's *Origin of Species* in 1859, 'The new conception of nature was complete in its main features . . . the whole of nature shown as moving in eternal flux and cycles.' He adds that man alone had succeeded in impressing his stamp on nature and, by better understanding the laws of nature, was capable of *reacting* to what he had done (ibid.: 74–5).

In the second essay, 'The Part Played by Labour in the Transition from Ape to Man', Engels expounds his view that economic growth need not damage man's harmony with nature. He remains an optimist: 'In fact, with every day that passes we are acquiring a better understanding of [nature's] laws and getting to perceive both the more immediate and the more remote consequences of our interference with the traditional course of nature' (Engels 1970b: 362). In Engels' view, our knowledge of science is the best guarantee that 'the natural consequences of at least our day-to-day production activities' are brought under control (ibid.: 362).

What remains interesting in this essay is Engels' recognition that man's mastery of nature *might* pose a threat to material advance itself. Engels suggests that man's ability to react to the changes he makes in his environment implies new responsibilities towards nature. In this he is well in advance of his time and, within Marxist thought, quite alone. The following passage represents, then, the closest thing to a 'conservation' approach in classical Marxist thought. In his insistence on man's need for caution in his treatment of the environment, Engels finds an echo in our time:

> Let us not, however, flatter ourselves overmuch on account of our human victories over nature. For each such victory nature takes its revenge on us . . . we are reminded that we by no means rule over nature, like someone standing outside nature, but that we . . . belong to nature, and exist in its midst, and that all over mastery of it consists in the fact that we have the advantage over all other creatures of being able to learn its laws and apply them correctly. (ibid.: 362)

Marx and Engels were principally concerned with the growth of capitalist industrial society. Not until the role of the geographical periphery was explored by Lenin, in his study of Russia's development at the close of the nineteenth century, was underdevelopment accorded serious attention (Lenin 1964). Lenin argued that the development of a market for capitalism's goods had two aspects: 'the development of capitalism in depth' − the centralized accumulation process − and 'the development of capitalism in breadth' − the extension of capitalist market relations to new territory (ibid.: 594). The internal trading relations that such a division gave rise to, and the exchange of agricultural products for finished manufactured goods, provided a model for a more generalizable 'world division of labour' (ibid.: 592). In his theory of imperialism Lenin gave fuller expression to this global view of underdevelopment, and helped to fire a contemporary debate (Lenin 1972).

IMPERIALISM AND RESOURCE USE ON THE PERIPHERY

The fallacy on which much development policy has been based is that the experience of the 'early industrializing countries', far from being historically specific, can be extrapolated to the countries of the periphery (Jones and Woolf 1969: 15). Shorn of 'developmentalist' bias the story runs rather differently. The early development of Western Europe necessitated the 'permanent occupation of the colonies' by the colonial powers, and the destruction of 'natural economy' (Luxemburg 1951: 371). Capitalism alienated the productive forces of 'natural economy' in a variety of ways, from market incorporation via primitive accumulation to violent seizure. The logic of the accumulation drive led, necessarily, to the destruction of simple exchange and the conversion of primitive societies into societies of 'commodity buyers' (Luxemburg 1951: 371). This scenario, described vividly by Rosa Luxemburg in Chapters 27 to 29 of *The Accumulation of Capital*, was often long drawn-out.

In the tropics the plantation economy was established to supply Europe with sugar, tobacco and other goods. However, another frontier was established in temperate latitudes, to be colonized by settlers able to exterminate the indigenous population and establish rapid autochthonous agricultural growth. This 'second' frontier gradually evolved an economic and social structure closer to that of Western Europe. Eventually, by the nineteenth century, mass production led to the growth of a large internal market. In North America particularly, an interdependence developed between agriculture and industry unlike anything that the plantation economy could provide (Jones and Woolf 1969: 19).

The terms of trade which developed between the colonial powers and their colonies were prejudicial to the latter's development. It was impossible for the capital accumulated in the colonies to be retained there, since merchant capital acted as the agency of the centre's interaction with the periphery. Not until this century has industrial capital been invested directly through the overseas firms of the ex-colonial powers, and the 'transnationalization' of capital seriously weakened the institutional links established with individual colonial powers. According to one interpretation, the history of underdevelopment is the history of 'merchant capital, [which] having lost out politically and economically to industrial capital in Europe, expanded its operations in the overseas empire' (de Silva 1982: 425). Thenceforth, merchant capital was to play a mediating role between pre-capitalist forms of production in the periphery and capitalism in the metropolis (ibid.: 426).

The colonial expansion marked the destruction of many village crafts, and although indigenous technology survived in the petty-commodity producing sector, this did not prevent the development of more advanced technologies. The growth of advanced agriculture, as well as industry, in the metropolitan states, further depressed the commodity selling power of the South. This dependence has only been weakened in recent times by the industrial countries' reliance on petroleum, but has not served to weaken the industrialized countries' hold on world commodity markets.

THE MODERNIZATION OF AGRICULTURE

It is useful to compare the 'political economy' approach to development with that of the 'modernization' school. Much of the economic literature on agricultural development, while paying meticulous attention to the supposed 'obstacles' to such development, makes only passing reference to the aims and objectives of 'development' itself. Clark and Haswell's classic text in agricultural economics provides numerous examples, of which the following will suffice:

> The normal and fortunate course of economic development is that, when the productivity of a country's agriculture can considerably exceed the required standards of consumption of the rural population, and when other circumstances are favourable too, urban and industrial population begins to grow.   (Clark and Haswell 1964: 137)

> As agricultural productivity increases this has two effects; first, everyone (agriculturists and non-agriculturists) has more to eat; secondly, an increasing proportion of the labour force can be diverted to non-agricultural activities.   (ibid.: 154)

The belief in equilibrium can hardly have been expressed better. In the real world, of course, urbanization often proceeds *together with* low levels of agricultural productivity and *despite* the fact that the basic needs of the poor are not met. Further, it is not at all clear, as the second quotation suggests, that increased agricultural productivity necessarily leads to improved nutritional standards; indeed the opposite effect has often been observed (Pearse 1980). The proportion of the labour force that 'can be diverted' (*sic*) to non-agricultural activities depends, initially, on the distribution of landholding and the labour absorbing capacities of industry, both of which are overlooked.

This kind of neoclassical analysis, depicting a 'normal' growth situation in which the factors of production are allocated in ways that maximize their productivity, still has adherents within agricultural economics. According to this view, agricultural development also failed in the South because physical compulsion of the labour force was incapable of stimulating the right sort of entrepreneurship (Hodder 1968: 52). Similarly, the imposition of heavier taxation on subsistence agriculture could be countenanced, despite misgivings, provided it led to the much vaunted transition from pure subsistence to a cash economy (Clark and Haswell 1964: 65). Social institutions in rural areas were evaluated in terms of their contribution, or supposed contribution (since evidence was not always forthcoming) to agricultural productivity. Difficulties were experienced where land was not 'a negotiable possession'; that is, it could not be sold. The absence of a land market suggested that 'the capital needs associated with the intensification of agricultural production' were not forthcoming (Hodder 1968: 121).

Other writers have proved more sceptical about the ability of social institutions to prevent agricultural growth. Some felt that land tenure was unlikely to prove a real barrier to development (Lewis 1955). Nevertheless, improved access to land was equally unlikely to increase agricultural efficiency (Bauer and Yamey 1957). At best, agricultural development proceeded despite social institutions; at worst, agricultural development necessitated some changes in these institutions (such as the private ownership of land) which would take the brake off development.

This metaphysical view of development has not been confined to economics. Sociology, in its functionalist phase, proved a willing handmaiden to positivist economic theory. As Apthorpe (1973) pungently observed, sociologists emphasized social barriers to economic development while ignoring economic barriers to social development. Among the corpus of sociological explanation current in the 1960s was Foster's 'image of limited good' and McClelland's investigation of the social psychology of achievement (Foster 1965, McClelland 1961). Peasant culture was antipathetic to development, because it emphasized harmony and equality and sought to restrict successful entrepreneurship. Hutton and Cohen, focusing on African material, were able to conclude that 'the explanations offered for peasants' economic strategies have been derived not from explanatory variables, but from a selection of dependent variables' (Hutton and Cohen 1975: 108).

Less far-fetched, and therefore more insistent, was the view that peasant communities operated 'levelling mechanisms' designed to reduce inequality and redistribute resources (Galjart 1979, Long 1977). They had thus solved the problem of how to distribute resources fairly. Like other explanations this view conferred an advantage on the sociologist that had previously rested on the economist; he was to be 'in possession of a kind of revealed knowledge' about the working of society (de Silva 1982: 4). The 'black box' that positivist economics had proposed for cultural traits and values was grabbed with alacrity by the sociologist and anthropologist.

The more that economists of the traditional stamp probed subsistence agriculture, the more confident they felt about criticizing the constraints imposed by existing land–labour ratios. Development was a linear process in which shifting field cultivation, labour using and capital saving, made way for permanent field cultivation and, through the stimulus of accelerating population, led to a feedback effect from industry. Crop research, pesticides, fertilizers, mechanization, roads and credit facilities all helped to develop an increasing labour-saving, capital-intensive agriculture. At this point it is assumed that population would begin to fall off. The model then suggested that the rapid feedback from industry into agriculture 'should be encouraged, emphasising from the start labour-saving, capital-intensive technology and making economic efficiency the sole criteria of judgement' (Hodder 1968: 168). The achievement of so elusive and harmonious a development path has proved difficult, although it has done little to quell the enthusiasm of its advocates. Marxist and neo-Marxist sociology, and the growing interest in political economy, have also taken their toll of adherents. Most significantly however – and this is a point to which we return below – indigenous agricultural systems, far from being dismissed as irrelevant or injurious to development, might in fact provide workable models of how to achieve a greater measure of equality without doing irreparable damage to the environment.

MARXIST DEVELOPMENT THEORY AND THE ENVIRONMENT

As we have seen, Marxist writing about the development process has accorded a secondary role to the natural environment. The reasons for this are not difficult to establish. In the development of the industrialized societies natural resources facilitated economic growth, but the unique contribution of capitalism lay in the way labour was employed in extended reproduction. Imperialism, which Lenin referred to as 'the highest stage in the development of capitalism', promised to reproduce these processes in the periphery (Lenin 1972). Although capitalism's penetration of the periphery was explained, logically, in terms of the contradictions imposed by capitalist development in the metropolitan countries, there was no suggestion in the writing of either Lenin or Rosa Luxemburg that, ultimately, peripheral capitalism would differ from metropolitan capitalism (Lenin 1972; Rosa Luxemburg 1951).

Rosa Luxemburg was in a position to appraise imperialism from a notable historical vantage point. The industrialized capitalist countries had completed their colonial thrust but had not yet been driven to war by the conflicting demands of empire. The 'invasion of primitive economies by capitalism' kept 'the system alive', as Joan Robinson remarked, but without the system having to be scrutinized for needed structural repairs (Luxemburg 1951: 26). The First World War and the Great Depression of the 1930s were to do that. In Luxemburg's writing we find a 'collapsed' view of imperialism, in which the early encounters with the New World and oriental civilization are bracketed together with the scramble for empire in the 1880s and 1890s.

Luxemburg's important contribution lies in the recognition that the very absence of development provided opportunities for capital accumulation that could not be provided in Europe:

> Only capital with its technical resources can effect such a miraculous change in so short a time – but only on the pre-capitalist soil of more primitive social conditions can it develop the ascendancy necessary to achieve such miracles. (Luxemburg 1951: 358)

For capital to become established in the periphery it was necessary to destroy the 'natural economy' that preceded it. The most important productive forces, 'the land, its hidden mineral treasure, and its meadows, woods and water', were only accessible through creating market conditions which would permit their sale (ibid.: 370). Natural economy was organized on the basis of use values and resisted penetration by capital. For capitalism to be established, commodity production had to be substituted for self-provisioning and simple exchange.

Luxemburg also recognized that the development of commodity production in colonial societies implied a basic contradiction in that, although capital needed pre-capitalist methods of production to sustain the accumulative drive, it could 'not tolerate their continued existence side by side with itself' (ibid.: 416). This contradiction has been the source of much of the current debate about the persistence and reproduction of petty-commodity production under peripheral capitalism. However, it did not lead to greater awareness of the part played by natural resources in the development process.

The 1960s marked a watershed in critical development theory. The Eurocentric bias implicit in the work of earlier Marxists like Lenin and Luxemburg had left a theoretical vacuum to be filled. At the same time, neoclassical approaches to development, by emphasizing the role of the market in restoring equilibrium to the world economy, seemed to promise continued poverty and exploitation for the less developed countries. What followed was a reconstruction of both Marxist and neoclassical theories.

Drawing on the revisionist Marxism of Paul Baran and the analysis of the ECLA (United Nations Economic Commission for Latin America) school in Latin America, André Gunder Frank redefined capitalist relations in peripheral countries, and set in motion a tidal wave of comment and controversy (Frank 1967, 1969; Laclau 1971; Cardoso 1972). The wider reaches of the sociology of development were enriched by the discussion which ensued (Bernstein 1973; Brookfield 1975; Oxaal et al. 1975; Long 1977; Roxborough 1979; Kitching 1982). The debate between Marxists was particularly animated, as 'unequal-exchange' theory gave way to 'articulation' theory, and 'post-articulation' writing sought new ways of conceptualizing the role of capital in development (Amin 1974; Emmanuel 1973; Godelier 1977; Bernstein 1977; Banaji 1977; Goodman and Redclift 1981). The growing literature in the sociology of development showed no signs of decline, especially as thorough, historically-delimited, country-based studies emerge to challenge the more sweeping generalizations in the theoretical literature (Kitching 1980; Leys 1977; Long and Roberts 1979; Lopes 1978). However, the focus of attention was still labour rather than natural resources.

Neoclassical development theory has also experienced difficulties in rising to the environmentalist challenge. A paradigm shift has not taken place, but 'mature' neoclassical theory has been broadened under the influence of economists interested in challenging the conventional wisdoms of much development theory, often by utilizing 'sociological' categories (Sen 1981; Bauer 1981). The major contribution to the development debate has come from the Brandt Committee's report, which makes a number of illuminating references to the part the destruction of the natural environment plays in the creation of rural poverty (Brandt 1980: 47, 73). Interestingly, as will be argued in the next chapter, the major report from the international agencies concerned specifically with the environment, the World Conservation Strategy, seems to have been written in total ignorance of Brandt's findings (World Conservation Strategy 1980). The view expressed in the World Conservation Strategy, held by the majority of international 'experts', and the Brandt approach have continued to run along parallel lines (Brandt 1983).

In the attempt to provide a firm historical basis to development theory, increasing attention has been paid to specific social formations, distinguishing between forms of peripheral underdevelopment. One such distinction in the political economy writing in recent years is that between 'settler' and 'non-settler' (or plantation) societies. It is worth asking whether this distinction is founded on environmental differences. Settler societies certainly tended to become established in areas where the population was relatively sparse, such as the East African Protectorates, much of South Africa and Algeria. In its most 'extreme' form settler societies were colonized by family farmers starved of land in Europe (examples of which include Canada, the west of the United States, New Zealand, Argentina and southern Brazil). In such societies land husbandry was practised without access to indigenous labour.

In the more common characterization of settler societies in Africa and Asia, however, access to indigenous labour was important. As de Silva notes, 'labour was a constant problem in settler societies' (1982: 144). Nevertheless, the permanent stake which European settlers had in their societies stimulated economic structures that were more viable than in plantation societies, and posed more of a challenge to the metropolitan states. Agriculture became more diversified, like that in the metropole, and development was orientated to *internal* markets, as well as for export. At the same time the relatively high level of wages and interest rates, together with the higher general level of prices (than in plantation societies) induced improved technology. By contrast, plantation societies, in which foreign investors confined themselves to trade, plantation crops and minerals, exhibited a strong anti-technological bias, maintaining coercive patterns of labour use and control.

Does such a characterization of peripheral capitalism assist us in exploring the relationship between political economy and the environment? In both cases, the environmental dimension in political economy can be identified, although it does not receive much attention. The principal difference in resource use between 'settler' and 'plantation' societies is that in the former the local environment was looked upon as a means of support by a privileged European élite. In 'plantation societies' the integration with metropolitan capital was closer, and the renewability of resources correspondingly less important, for the small resident class of expatriate Europeans.

The nearer we come to an analysis of specific social formations in the periphery, the less apposite is the model derived from European experience of resource use under capitalism. In the 'orthodox' view the environment can be expected to fare as it had in the industrialized countries, but the difficulty this presents is that imperialism has been a long drawn-out process implying, at different stages, plunder, the introduction of private property in land, the eradication of competitive native industry, and the search for new raw materials for processing in the industrialized countries (Magdoff 1982: 18). In some Latin American countries for example, the development of an internal market and rapid urban expansion have precipitated new forms of international exchange and attracted considerable capital investment from multinational companies. Contrary to expectation such processes co-exist with, and are supported by, petty-commodity production in agriculture. The environmental problems attributable to the development process thus include both industrial pollution in the cities and soil erosion in the countryside. The environment of rural areas is impoverished by the way urban and industrial accumulation proceeds, leading to situations in the cities not unlike, although qualitatively often worse than, those in the urban capitals of Europe, North America and Japan.

The lack of definition in the political economy approach to the environment requires explanation. At one level it is curious that those who believe the material conditions of production are a determining factor in the development of society should devote so little attention to the resources, especially land, on which relations of production are constructed. Although the ownership of capital and the disruptive effects of capital penetration in the Third World have been explored at length and reviewed at even more length (Roberts 1978; Gutkind and Waterman 1977; Heyer, Roberts and Williams 1981; Harriss 1981), the implications of technology's use of natural resources, and the effects of the disruption of traditional ecosystems on the production process, have received little attention from Marxists. Nor is this *lacuna* confined to the micro-level of village or farm. The international dimension of the problem has also been particularly badly served. Most social scientists have confined their attention to trade relations, investment policies and the transfer of industrial technology. The conversion of vegetable into animal protein for consumption in the developed countries, and the high income markets of some less developed countries, has attracted little attention from theorists of underdevelopment, despite its importance in distributional terms. Similarly, the heavy dependence of modern agriculture on inanimate energy subsidies in the form of fertilizers, fuel and processing plant carries a cost that is paid principally by the oil-poor developing world. By contrast, in most developing countries agricultural sectors 'are net energy producers – that is, the kilocalories of food produced exceed the kilocalories of inanimate energy subsidy' (Buttel 1979: 1). Another way of looking at the implications of the developed countries' agricultures is to reflect that if all the countries in the world (industrialized and non-industrialized) used as much energy to feed themselves as the non-industrialized countries do at present they would use only 40 per cent of total world energy consumption (Leach 1976).

Underdevelopment is not just an effect of capital's rapaciousness; it is an effect of our consumption habits and the technologies used to feed these habits. However, consciousness of this important dimension has not permeated the writing of many who approach development issues from the standpoint of 'political economy'. A study like that of Norman Myers, which documents the way in which natural species are in danger of disappearing in the face of the combined efforts of multinationals and international food policies, effectively lays down the gauntlet to the social scientists versed in the approach of political economy (Myers 1979).

Among those who have addressed these kinds of distributional issues is the 'Food First' school of writers on development (Lappé and Collins 1977). On the other hand, Marxist writing on resources and the environment from within a political economy perspective is hardly less distinguished than when Foster-Carter drew attention to it over a decade ago (Foster-Carter 1974; Caldwell 1977). In a far-sighted essay, Foster-Carter identified the reasons for concentrating on the environment in the developing countries. He suggested that the way natural resources are being depleted in the drive to industrialization and the 'modernization' of agriculture casts doubt on the sustainability of development in both rich *and* poor countries. He argues, quoting Caldwell's seminal work, that 'not just capitalist underdevelopment but industrial society as such, must now be seen as an historical cul-de-sac, and that further social development will come from a stage "further back"' (Foster-Carter 1974: 93; Caldwell 1977).

If we take the view of most political economy writers today, that capitalist industrialization proceeds through destroying natural resources in the periphery but *without* causing an imminent global resource crisis, then an ecological perspective remains something of a luxury. If, however, we take the view, eloquently expressed by Caldwell, that 'transcending' both underdevelopment *and* overdevelopment requires that we 'fully appreciate . . . the objective natural limits to our manipulation of our environment', then we must begin to question the utility of a perspective on development which places so little emphasis on resources and the environment (Caldwell 1977).

To summarize, this chapter has argued for a fundamental revision in Marxist political economy, to reflect the urgency of the South's environmental crisis. First, it was suggested that environmental consciousness was itself an important element in the ideological superstructure of modern society and, as such, capable of influencing the pursuit of economic growth. Second, it was argued that the role of science and technology in development was more problematical than Marx and the early Marxists envisaged. Human society's urgent need to control its own technology and to develop more socially beneficial technology is an important element in environmentalist thinking, but tends to be treated as a dependent variable in political economy. Third, underdevelopment can no longer be represented largely in terms of the way labour is exploited in dependent capitalist countries. In these countries natural resources are systematically depleted in the accumulation drive by both private multinational capital and the state. Ecological degradation in the South assumes emergency proportions largely through the mindless commitment to the economic growth strategy endemic to developed capitalism. The costs of development are expressed not only in terms of class conflict and economic exploitation, but also in the reduction of the natural resource base on which the poor depend for their livelihoods. For political economy to ignore this process it must forfeit the claim to be explanatory. In the next chapter the evidence for the global resource crisis is presented, and attention is directed at the new forms of environmental degradation being forced upon the South.

2

Global resource problems

It has been argued that political economy needs considerable rethinking if our understanding of underdevelopment is to reflect the resource crisis facing the South. The concentration on economic growth which played such a formative role in the development of classical economic theory also left an indelible mark on Marxism. The deficiencies of underdevelopment theory can be appreciated, however, in ways that are practical as well as theoretical. The gulf that exists between our understanding of environmental change in developing countries, and holistic development theory, is matched by an equally important gulf between the identification of environmental problems and the implementation of workable policies to ensure their solution.

This chapter considers the evidence that the world's natural resources, particularly land, biomass and water supplies, are so imperilled by the development process that 'development' itself is put in jeopardy. Beginning with an examination of the factors which lead us to ignore or seriously misrepresent the South's environmental crisis, the discussion links these ideological processes with the processes of resource depredation itself. In the final section attention is focused on the way in which agribusiness development has placed short-term commercial gains before rural development and the conservation of the natural environment.

Present development policy seriously exacerbates the environmental problems that accompany resource depletion in the developing countries. Choices in development models exist which would permit a sustainable development, but they are not widely canvassed in the industrialized countries and would necessitate some uncomfortable changes in expectations and demand. The limits on international society's ability to solve environmental problems are not technical but political and economic, many of them stemming from the structure of demand in the developed countries and their relations with the underdeveloped world. This is particularly true of much needed measures for environmental protection (Global 2000 1982: 229).

The view that we take of the natural environment is similar to the commonly-held assumptions about 'natural disasters' of all kinds. The boundaries between the 'social' and the 'natural' are not at all clear cut. Evidence from the study of disaster relief suggests that social factors are a major element in a society's vulnerability to 'natural' disasters (Jeffery 1981). Similarly, as we shall see in Chapter 4, studies indicate clearly that failures in the supply of food are not the principal cause of famine, but the inadequate demand for food among particularly vulnerable groups. Changes in income distribution and lower absolute income levels can provoke widespread famine even when harvests are average (Sen 1981).

[margin note: not physical / social.]

Responsiveness to poverty involves finding ways of reducing the cumulative effects of natural forces and social deprivation. Recent studies of health and nutrition in the South show that it would be possible to reduce hardship among vulnerable groups, especially women and children, if more attention was paid to seasonal factors in tropical agriculture (Chambers 1981). Concern with the role of women in development has highlighted the need to gain a better understanding of target groups in rural development planning (Nelson 1979; Rogers 1981). In each of these areas – disaster relief, famine, seasonality, women – current resource uses have differential effects on society. The environment, often perceived simply in terms of 'natural' forces, helps to shape social relations and the life chances of the population.

[margin note: environ dualism / shape the society]

The accumulative drive that is necessary to satisfy the consumer demands of the North's population, and that part of the South's population which has become accustomed to similar consumption habits, exacts a high price both in terms of the depletion of resources, and the creation of waste. 'Development' is sustained by economic ideology rather than resources. Looked at in this way GNP 'is a measure of decay (of food, clothing, gadgets and gasoline) and the bigger the economic system the more it decays and the more that has to be produced simply to maintain it' (Simmons 1974: 354). Most developed countries are geared to resource utilization rather than resource conservation.

THE MYSTIFICATION OF ENVIRONMENTAL VALUES

Before considering the ways in which current global economic relations prejudice sustainable development and dictate the pattern of resource use in the less developed countries, it is important to identify those factors that limit our ability to respond effectively to these uses. We can identify at least four ways in which societies are prevented from elaborating effective environmental policies through the mystification of environmental values.

First, the development of 'high technology' and the international division of labour lead us to ignore the links between the 'causes' and 'effects' of resource depletion, because of the priority given to our own physiological and psychological needs. For example, we are seldom aware when we buy canned dogfood in a supermarket that meeting this market need assumes as much importance in producer countries as improvements in the human diet. Various factors conspire to reduce our awareness: the advertising on behalf of the manufacturer, the geographical distance between the food's origin and its consumption, even the extent to which we are led to feel responsibility for poverty in other societies. Inasmuch as the media give attention to the relationship between eating habits and nutrition, it is *our* nutrition that is the object of attention, not that of those millions of people in the South whose land use is dictated by production and marketing strategies in the developed North.

A second source of mystification is what economists term 'externalities': that is, the environmental costs that are not included in the market price of a commodity or service. Since we do not possess a tangible means of weighing the environmental costs of using herbicides on crops or emitting lead with car exhaust fumes, the negative aspects of these processes can easily be ignored. The methodologies of environmental scientists have been predicated upon the need to measure and quantify these 'externalities' more rigorously.

Third, resource misuse or depletion involves questions of intergenerational equity which are rarely, if ever, considered in policy discussions. In most societies future benefits and costs of protecting the environment are valued less (that is, they are discounted) relative to current benefits and costs. Conservation and environmental protection become more difficult the higher the discount rate (Arrow 1976). Competitiveness in market economies and bureaucratic inertia in socialist ones tend to work against equalizing effects over the longer term.

Lastly, and returning to a point that was made in the previous chapter, our ability to respond effectively to the environmental consequences of resource use is seriously impaired by each society's commitment to its own ideology of economic growth. The political risks in breaking with dominant ideological formulations of growth are frequently greater than shifts along a Left/Right axis, since they imply a major departure from existing technologies, patterns of consumption and, perhaps most importantly, social values. Although in the United Kingdom we have entered a 'low growth' period, this has not yet stimulated a re-examination of the resource implications of de-industrialization in our own country. It remains to be seen whether long-term unemployment, enforced leisure and the burgeoning 'black economy' will serve to make us more environmentally conscious in the future. The patterns of resource use to which we shall refer in this chapter (of energy, water and land) are dictated by current economic demand in the North, as well as economic relations with the South. These underlying patterns underpin the distributional policies of both left- and right-wing governments in the industrialized countries. One movement which has organized to reverse these policies through a departure from current growth orthodoxy is the European Green Movement. The philosophy of the Greens is subjected to scrutiny in Chapter 3.

GLOBAL RESOURCES AND THE INTERNATIONAL ECONOMY

Economic relations between developed and developing countries contribute to environmental problems in a number of ways. First, each individual in industrial society makes larger demands on the world's resources than does each individual in the less developed countries. It is intellectually dishonest to attribute the global resource crisis to the population explosion in the less developed countries, without acknowledging that the share of resources consumed by poor people in these countries is much smaller *per capita* than it is in a country like Britain.

Second, the satisfaction of our own economic demands in the industrialized countries cannot be met solely from our own resource base. To a significant extent, the resource and environmental pressures felt in the South are linked to high living standards and wasteful resource use in the North. The market economies of the developed countries contribute to poverty while imperilling attempts at finding a solution to resource depletion. Physical distance and the ideological biases of consumer society prevent us from drawing radical inferences from our consumption of goods and its manipulation by the mass media.

Third, industrial societies are notorious in not being able to recycle discarded waste, with consequences that are both environmentally and socially damaging. In the United States, for example, industrial solid wastes generated in 1977 totalled about 344 million metric tons. The average person there produced about 1300 lbs of municipal solid waste annually (Global 2000 1982: 239). The cost of disposing of this waste is high, many materials that could be recycled are not, and an opportunity is lost to generate employment around the 'informal' economic activities associated with waste disposal. Although recycling processes may be expensive in energy they use cheap raw materials and abundant labour. In many less developed countries rubbish tips are an important source of raw materials and an area of intense entrepreneurial activity (Bromley and Gerry 1979). In Brazil, for example, more useful employment is probably generated from refashioning discarded vehicle tyres than from their original productive use.

The prescription for change in the international economy is usually more North–South investment. In recent years the demands of the South that their economic interests be protected in trade relations with the North have also been widely discussed, culminating in the Third World Summit at Cancún in December 1981. However, the 'unequal exchange' between North and South is not simply between the rich countries and the poor (Emmanuel 1973; Amin 1974). As the Brandt Report made clear, 70 per cent of capital investment in the Third World, excluding the 'tax havens', was confined to only fifteen countries, and over 20 per cent was in Brazil and Mexico alone. Most of the capital investment was in other middle-income countries like Argentina, Venezuela, Malaysia, Singapore and Hong Kong or in the oil-exporting countries (Brandt 1980: 188). Investment is not helping to develop the poorer countries; it is seeking out markets for its products in those which are partially developed and helping to restructure international capital in the process. It may be true, as Brookfield suggests, that the scarcity of natural resources is of less importance than their immobility (Brookfield 1975: 205). Nevertheless, the immobility of natural resources is not an obstacle to their destruction today, any more than it was under natural economy. Resource location does not deter capital from seeking new forms of penetration. The logic of transnational companies is precisely the logic of the so-called new technologies, for which the location of resources, human as well as natural, presents no barriers. Indeed, difficulty of geographical access to natural resources confers advantages on transnationals by virtue of their size and international character.

One example of this trend is the siting of 'assembly shops' in areas that border the developed North like Mexico and Taiwan. Here manufactured components are assembled into finished goods by cheap, mainly female, labour. The growing literature on 'assembly shops' suggests that their effect on local labour markets is by no means universally beneficial and they do not have a wider 'multiplier' effect on the economies of the host country (Redclift 1982; Kelly 1980). Labour, a resource which is at the disposal of all Third World countries, is used to buttress existing economic inequalities, while both energy and raw materials are diverted towards satisfying the demand for high technology goods in the rich countries.

The balance of advantages between North and South is dictated not only by the commercial objectives of transnational companies based in the industrialized world, it is also dictated by the technologies which such companies command and the research facilities that enable them to both generate products *and* manipulate the demand for them. The effects of these technological processes are often felt at several removes from their consumption, in the way natural resources are converted. Crops such as soya are processed for consumption in the North or, like sorghum, fed to animals in the South, again for eventual export to the developed markets. The way in which petroleum is processed for use as fertilizers and insecticides in developed country agriculture is also a case in point, as we shall see later in this chapter. Just as the developed countries have long refined mineral ores extracted from less developed countries, today they increasingly import primary products for reprocessing in their own countries.

FOREST AND ENERGY RESOURCES

human construction.

Deforestation, especially in the humid tropics, provides a good example of the way that resource depletion is only recognized as a 'problem' when it reaches crisis proportions, and only then because it is associated with overpopulation and a lack of environmental consciousness among the rural poor (Plumwood and Routley 1982). Such an interpretation is seriously misleading, but an effective rebuttal requires careful documentation.

The scale of deforestation and its ecological consequences can hardly be exaggerated. Myers estimates that each year 200,000 square kilometres of tropical moist forest is lost to commercial logging and 'follow-on' cultivating (Myers 1979: 174). By the year 2,020 virtually all of the physically accessible forest in the South will have disappeared (Global 2000 1982: 26). Although the total world forest area will have stabilized, much as the industrialized nations' forest area has already stabilized at 1.5 billion hectares (ha), most of the damage will already have been done.

The picture is bleak wherever one looks in the South. It is estimated that only 30 per cent of the original forest is left in the Philippines, that the forest of West Africa will have been exploited to the point of extinction by the end of the century, while lowland forest depletion in peninsular Malaya has reached crisis proportions (Meijer 1980: 203). In Mexico the forests of Chiapas are being 'mined' to make way for cattle-ranching. Between 1950 and 1970 the tropical forested area of that country was halved. In the mid-1970s, according to the United Nations, tropical moist forests covered about 935 million ha. They had already been reduced from their natural area by 40 per cent. The annual rate of deforestation in Latin America at the end of the 1970s was estimated to be about 4.2 million ha a year. This compares with about 1.3 million ha in Africa and 1.8 million ha in Asia. The retreat of the world's tropical forests was estimated to be 7.3 million ha a year, or 14 ha a minute (Eckholm 1982: 159).

There are clear environmental costs in making excessive demands on the tropical forests. In the tropical forests most of the nutrients are held in the biomass rather than the soils, which are relatively poor. Shifting cultivation was viable only when secondary forest was left to regenerate. Thus the removal of biomass, and the changes in the soil, threaten the very environment which made the tropical forests highly productive. 'As a result, agricultural yields, which are often rather low, particularly in Africa, quickly fall and deforestation proceeds faster still' (Longman and Jenik 1974: 120).

The effects are not confined to lowland tropical forests. Ecological damage in one area often carries consequences for other, adjacent, areas. Fragile areas, often with steep slopes and erodible soils, are also the source areas for major rivers. Watershed forests in such areas are of critical importance. As expressed in the World Conservation Strategy:

> Only 10% of the world's population live in mountainous areas but another 40% live in the adjacent plains; so the lives and livelihoods of half the world directly depend on the way in which watershed ecosystems are managed.
> (WCS 1980)

As the moist tropical forests disappear, the attention of logging companies is likely to be increasingly diverted to the montane, or highland forests. In areas like southern Sumatra and Malaysia, these forests are already under threat, with dire consequences for water regimes in neighbouring ecological zones as well as longer-term distortions in the climate.

The importance of steep-sloped areas not only for forestry but for crops makes their protection an urgent priority. It has been estimated that 30 per cent of agricultural families in tropical Central and South America live in areas of this kind (Posner and McPherson 1981: 4). In the highlands limited access to good land and increasing population 'will expand the cultivation of the more marginal lands, shorten fallow rotations, and reduce the amount of land per farm family' (ibid.: 16). Posner and McPherson conclude that the problems of steep-sloped areas in the tropics are compounded by the priority which development agencies attach to assisting other, more 'productive' locations, and thus shifting the burden of poverty further towards the endangered upland environments.

The depletion of forest resources has distributive consequences that are only vaguely recognized by international conservation agencies. In most of the poorest countries the principal sources of energy are wood and animal dung rather than oil. The rapidity of deforestation in these countries thus presents a threat to the immediate viability of populations dependent upon agriculture. The South contains nearly half the world's forest area and over half of the timber-growing stock. Apart from providing essential fuel these timber resources play an important role in providing shelter, creating employment and contribute importantly to the maintenance of subsistence farming systems. Increasingly, large amounts of time are spent in finding fuel and transporting it. Fuel wood is so scarce in the Gambia that gathering it takes 360 woman days a year per family (FAO 1978). In Nepal, parts of the Andes and the African Sahel, the labour-time devoted to fuel-wood collection seriously disrupts household production (FAO 1978). In marginal areas, increased shrub and tree cutting impose an additional burden on already poor environments.

The fuel-wood problem has often been stated without adequate regard being paid to the relationship between the production and consumption processes. Gamser argues that little work has been undertaken 'to identify rural energy-use patterns in research on forest resources' (1980: 770). Most of the wood that is cut and gathered for domestic use in developing countries goes unrecorded in national statistics. The actual levels of fuel-wood consumption and production are likely to be much higher than suggested by official figures. Although, as Gamser suggests, social surveys of villages to establish the rate of fuel-wood depletion are difficult to design and implement, they can be extremely illuminating. The conversion of wood resources to charcoal for urban consumption is a case in point. This conversion reduces firewood availability in rural areas. As Gamser puts it, 'urban energy development proceeds at the expense of rural resource needs' (1980: 772). In one study near Mexico City charcoal production for village barbecues frequented by visitors and weekend tourists accounted for much of the fuel wood consumed in one village. In another village, further from the city, each household spent an average of nine hours a week gathering 12 kg of wood. In the two villages studied, over 80 per cent of households possessed gas stoves for cooking, but the cost of using gas was prohibitive for poor households (Cuanalo 1983: 10). In Mexico natural gas and petroleum reserves are vast, but the cost of denying the rural poor cheap gas supplies is paid by the natural environment, especially in rural areas near large urban populations.

Fuel-wood depletion is everywhere associated with the undervalued labour of women and children. As increasing quantities of charcoal are required for urban consumption, rural women and children have to spend greater amounts of time gathering firewood. It is in this sense that we must pose the problem not in terms of whether or not there is an energy crisis, but rather, *whose* energy crisis it is (Gamser 1980: 772).

In areas where the lumber industry and cattle-ranching are important, wood losses are attributable to commercial pressures rather than household fuel consumption. According to official figures from Brazil, during the period 1966–75 the colonization programme undertaken by peasant farmers cleared 17.6 per cent of the total area deforested. By contrast, large-scale cattle-raising projects and the highway construction programme of the Brazilian government accounted for more than 60 per cent of forest losses (Plumwood and Routley 1982: 7). The large corporate ranchers operating in the Amazon have nevertheless been able to lay the blame for deforestation in the Amazon on the peasant colonizers, most of whom eventually find themselves ejected from the land they have cleared.

The failure of most governments and international agencies to take action to reduce deforestation, logging and cattle-ranching in the South is explained by the concern to generate foreign exchange and the assistance given to these processes by major funding from international development banks. One example is the plan to flood large areas of the Amazon Basin to provide hydropower, a plan which promised to destroy huge areas of forest, and was thought up by the Hudson Institute (Plumwood and Routley 1982: 20). The 1970s was 'a decade of uncontrolled development activities' in the Brazilian Amazon, and 'very few lessons learned before the 1970s were taken into consideration as planners instituted projects that overlooked Amazonian realities' (Moran 1982: 28). The realities that were not overlooked were those of the transnational companies involved in exploiting the resource potential of the region for private, short-term gain.

The differential effect of deforestation, imperilling the livelihoods of many of the rural poor, while enriching ranchers and lumber companies, has led some commentators to take increasingly radical positions. The absence of concrete information on the activities of logging and corporate interests is seen as neither accidental nor unavoidable (Plumwood and Routley 1982: 19). Within some sections of the forestry profession dissent has also broken out, the advocates of conservation arguing that 'foresters the world over have had inculcated in them the belief that all values should be reduced to money values' (Meijer 1980: 203). Thus, to orthodox foresters planted forests are more valuable than native or regenerated forests, although not to conservationists. Meijer, one of the foremost critics of the market ideology in forestry, criticizes the absence of any political analysis in the international concern over tropical forest depletion. He deplores the tendency to regard the competing claims of timber concession holders, shifting cultivators and transmigrants as equally valid (Meijer 1980: 204).

Global deforestation needs to be related to wider issues of resource development, affecting not only the equilibrium of fragile environments and the livelihood of poor rural households, but also the share of the earth's resources which is consumed by the rich industrial countries. Economic development is highly dependent, at present, upon oil and natural gas. The available evidence suggests that oil production cannot keep pace with demand this century (Global 2000 1982: 171). Even technological changes to other sources of energy – solar, wind, geothermal and nuclear 'will not cover the excess of United States energy demand over supply' (ibid.: 172). At the same time the newly industrializing countries are placing increased demands on available oil resources. The challenge for the developed countries lies not only in shifting to other forms of

Table 1 Energy consumption *per capita* in the twenty most populous countries, 1974*

	Kg of coal equivalent
United States	11,485
Federal Republic of Germany	5,689
United Kingdom	5,464
USSR	5,252
France	4,330
Japan	3,839
Italy	3,227
Spain	2,063
Mexico	1,269
Brazil	646
People's Republic of China	632
Turkey	628
Egypt	322
Philippines	309
Thailand	300
India	201
Pakistan	188
Indonesia	158
Nigeria	94
Bangladesh	31

* Excludes firewood and dung
Source: Lester R. Brown (1978) *The Twenty-Ninth Day*, New York, Norton, p. 202.

energy, but in adopting much more effective oil conservation policies. Future projections of global supply, even on the optimistic assumption that the OPEC countries continue to release oil and natural gas on the same scale as at present, suggest serious energy shortages before the end of this century.

The rapid depletion of energy resources is attributable to development models that are wasteful as well as inequitable. As Table 1 shows, the *per capita* consumption of energy in the United States is ten times that of Brazil and three hundred times that of Bangladesh (Brown 1978: 202). Alternative sources of energy have been neglected because of petroleum's relative 'cheapness' and the ease with which it can be used. The rich countries' market preferences have thus had a distorting effect on resource use and the development of more conservationist energy policies. On the one hand, the industrial countries' demand for hydrocarbons seriously weakens the industrial growth potential of some countries in the South. On the other hand, the poor countries face increasing environmental pressure from corporate interests based in the North, whose activities have seriously depleted the world's forest resources and helped to push poor rural people on to marginal land where they are unable to break out of the cycle of environmental poverty.

WATER RESOURCES

Water is necessary to the performance of most productive activities in human society, but water is rarely analysed sociologically despite important historical precedents, notably Wittfogel (1957). Water is withdrawn from the surface and ground for domestic use, industry, crop irrigation and energy production. The distribution of water withdrawals among these uses varies markedly depending upon the level of industrialization, standard of living and the use which agriculture makes of irrigation. Countries as unlike as India, Mexico and Bulgaria all devote most of their water supplies to agriculture, while the United Kingdom, Poland and West Germany are geared principally to supplying industry. Some industrialized countries, like Japan, persist in devoting most of their water supply to agriculture (Global 2000 1982: 142).

The differences in *per capita* water consumption between the richest and the poorest countries are much less than those for energy resources, principally because of the important role of irrigation in many parts of Asia. However, forecasts of future water withdrawals rest upon various determinants of water demand including future lifestyles, family income, family size and water-using appliance technology. The heavy dependence of many poor countries on irrigated agriculture has led to political measures favourable to irrigation, especially the subsidizing of irrigation water. One effect of these subsidies has been to divert water into relatively wasteful irrigation practices without combating widespread ignorance of more efficient irrigation technologies.

Irrigation, however necessary or desirable it may be, often reinforces inequality in the less developed countries (van der Velde 1980). It is important not to gloss over the specific ways in which this happens. In South Asia it is often weak corporate organization in 'tail-end villages' (those at the end of the pipelines) which enables large farmers to divert water resources to their own benefit (Wade 1979: 15). Water technology also provides opportunities for entrepreneurship which have important distributive consequences. Ahmed (1975) has shown how those who could afford to buy handpumps rented them out to small farmers and sharecroppers. In the Kosi region of India, Clay (1980) has described how benefits from bamboo tubewells are diverted away from the poorer groups. In much of South Asia the control over water exercised by bureaucracies has enabled them to wield considerable political power. As Wade remarks, 'it is likely that elective institutions have amplified the pressures towards corruption and made it more systematic' (1982: 318). Thus politicians help meet the cost of electoral competition by relying on the irrigation bureaucracy to reward political supporters, and irrigation officials receive 'kickbacks' from large farmers and politicians for services rendered. The collective interests of large farmers 'seem to correspond rather closely with the . . . performance of the canal bureaucracy' (ibid.: 288). Similar distributive consequences of irrigation systems have been documented for other areas of Asia (Biggs and Burns 1976; Biggs 1981).

The possibility of making dramatic gains in agricultural production from irrigated agriculture has also proved a source of inequity in countries where most peasant farmers live in the unirrigated, rain-fed regions. Mexico is a case in point. As will be discussed in Chapter 5, the irrigated areas of north and north-west Mexico have received a disproportionate amount of public investment, leading to increased social differentiation and landlessness, while the bulk of poor rural households who live in the highland region have benefited little from improved technology, agricultural credit or technical assistance (Hewitt 1976; Redclift 1981). In north-east Brazil the alleviation of drought, sought by the government agency SUDENE (The Superintendency for the Development of the North East), did little to improve risk-taking of poor farmers, while assisting the penetration of transnational capital (Oliveira 1981).

Much of the African continent suffers from a serious shortage of water.

As a result the choice of priorities in the allocation of water, between valley or lake development (Senegal, Niger, Zambezi, Chad) or the irrigation of many smaller areas on the perimeter of major water supplies is an important political issue (UNEP 1981: 8). Choices over the exploitation and management of underground water resources and irrigation schemes are linked to pressures in favour of cash-crop farming rather than the production of food staples. Frequently the livelihoods of poor rural households, with little political power, are sacrificed to agribusiness interests and large farmers (Dinham and Hines 1983). The supremacy of professionals concerned with water management within rural development is well illustrated by Shepherd from Sudanese material:

> Organisationally water supplies have been the core of the succession of bodies set up to deal with rural development. With brief interludes, the sheer provision of water has dominated rural development. Professionally, engineers and hydrogeologists have dominated agriculturalists and land specialists associated with rural development. Since [water supply was separated from rural development in 1975] . . . rural development has sunk back to a lower level priority.
>
> (Shepherd 1982: 24)

The provision of drinking water is another area in which allocation follows social inequalities. The quality of drinking water is closely associated with the incidence of disease. Those African countries where at least 72 per cent of the population do not have safe drinking water are also those where the rate of infant mortality is equal to or greater than 160 per 1000 (UNEP 1981: 25). Urban areas are more likely to have safe drinking water than rural areas, where only 21 per cent of the population was adequately supplied with water in 1975. Almost half the cost of improving water provision has been financed by foreign aid, and is particularly vulnerable to economies when African countries face mounting food deficits, which also need to be financed.

The UNEP report already cited makes explicit the link between the major hydro-agricultural projects in Africa (Senegal, Niger, Nile) and the benefits derived from them by agribusiness. It also records the ecological consequences of an extension of irrigated argribusiness development, including the depletion of soils, deforestation and other damage to the fragile environment of the affected regions (UNEP 1981: 29). Environmental consequences of existing water uses are also important. Water pollution from heavy application of pesticides will increase, especially in those countries where the largest increases in agricultural chemical use will take place (Bull 1982). Irrigation also adversely affects water quality by adding salt to the water returning to streams and rivers, unless expensive desalinization measures are undertaken. Urbanization will exacerbate these problems and those of human waste disposal. River basin development combining flood control, the generation of electricity and irrigation can damage both freshwater and coastal ecosystems (Global 2000 1982: 35).

In considering both the use to which existing water resources are put and the social consequences of developing new water resources, we need to be aware of the relationship between the gains in economic power that accrue to some classes and the social deprivation which faces others. Projects that are superficially beneficial from a welfare standpoint, such as groundwater irrigation, might disguise important shifts in the control of resources from the poor to the rich, or from the country to the city. The location of water resources in nature does not correspond to the distribution of social need anywhere on the globe. However, these natural 'inequalities' are exaggerated by the social structural re-allocation of water resources in favour of those with more economic power and political leverage.

AGRIBUSINESS AND FOOD PRODUCTION

The use to which land is put depends on the social classes which own or control it. It has been suggested that a mere 2.5 per cent of landowners with holdings of more than 250 acres control nearly three-quarters of the earth's land resources (Norton-Taylor 1982: 296). Such figures can be challenged, but they do point to an issue which has continued to animate much of the world's population: the fact that to many people the concentration of landholding appears contrary to laws of natural justice. Inequalities in the ownership and control of land, where they are recognized, provoke more radical responses than inequalities in other resources, from neopopulist demands for land reform to demands for land nationalization (Lehmann 1978). We turn to the question of land distribution in Chapter 4.

Land distribution helps account for the persistence of rural poverty. For the present we are interested in the effect of land concentration on the use that is made of land resources. Specifically, to what extent does agribusiness make a contribution to food production and development? The answer to this question is more complicated than might initially appear.

We can make a start at analysing the problem by looking at 'food destinations': the way in which the food that is produced in the South arrives in the supermarkets or stores of large cities throughout the world. The companies that process food are not necessarily large landowners in the less developed countries. Del Monte, the United States-based fruit and canning company, owns farms and factories in over twenty countries. Nestlé, on the other hand, has become the world's second largest food company without owning a single cow or acre of coffee or cocoa plantation. To see how Nestlé operates in the South we need to study the introduction of dairying to parts of highland Ecuador, or the Cajamarca valley in Peru where Nestlé has made a significant impact on the production activities of 'subsistence' peasant farmers (Archetti 1977). The food chain stretches from Andean villages to the high street supermarket.

The food that reaches the supermarkets is rarely produced by peasant farmers. Nor is it making a significant contribution to meeting the needs of the vast majority of poor people in urban areas. Food needs are not met because food fails to get to the right people. At the global level it remains true that current food production, if equitably distributed, would feed the world's population quite adequately (King 1980: 29).

The question of food distribution is complicated by the fact that the *kind* of food produced is influenced by its consumption. Thus, most of the cereal production in the South is consumed directly by human beings but as people in the richer countries eat more meat an increasing proportion of it is being diverted into animal feeds. Only 10 per cent of world grain production is consumed directly; the rest of the carbohydrate is converted to protein through the inefficient medium of livestock (King 1980: 30). As development proceeds, the meat protein consumed in the poorer countries, mainly by the richer people, takes a larger slice out of the cereal availability there (see Table 2). The global growth in food production that has kept ahead of population growth fairly consistently, except in Africa, has been used to support affluent eating habits in the North. In the balance that has to be struck between foreign exchange earnings and domestic food needs, the process of land conversion by agribusiness exerts a powerful influence. Among the aspects of this process that deserve careful attention are the effect of agribusiness development on existing food provisioning in underdeveloped countries, and the effect of agribusiness on the rural environments of these countries.

The advocates of agribusiness see it as an extension to the South of developed country experience. Agribusiness means an integrated food system, linking farm to factory, and factory to consumer. The link between agriculture and industry is not merely one of vertical integration, however. Agricultural production increasingly 'resembles industrial production in the application of technology to control nature . . . and in the use of wage labour' (Burbach and Flynn 1980: 12).

Table 2 Annual grain consumption *per capita* in the twenty most populous countries, 1975*

	Kg
United States	708
USSR	645
Spain	508
France	446
Federal Republic of Germany	441
Turkey	415
Italy	413
United Kingdom	394
Mexico	304
Egypt	286
Japan	274
Brazil	239
Thailand	225
People's Republic of China	218
Bangladesh	203
Pakistan	171
Philippines	157
Indonesia	152
India	150
Nigeria	92

* Includes grain consumed both directly and indirectly (in the form of meat, milk and eggs).
Source: Lester R. Brown (1978) *The Twenty-Ninth Day*, New York, Norton, p. 200.

The technology employed, as well as the marketing systems and advertising campaigns, is that of the multinational corporations based in the industrialized countries.

Capitalist agriculture in Latin America has advanced further, and with more dramatic effect, than in other parts of the third world. Latin America's geographical proximity to the United States confers on agribusiness a series of locational and political advantages. Most governments in Latin America tacitly accept the economic hegemony of the United States and its commitment to a model of economic development based upon large-scale, capital-intensive production units. The effect, as Burbach and Flynn note, is that the emerging agrarian bourgeoisie is increasingly similar in North and South America:

In the Bajio Valley of Mexico, the Cauca Valley of Colombia, and the Salinas Valley of California we saw fruit and vegetable growers who employed similar production techniques. They used the same hybrid seeds, bought the same farm implements, and applied the same fertilisers and pesticides. They were financed by the same banks, and sold to the same multinational corporations.

(Burbach and Flynn 1980: 15)

Agribusiness in Latin America not only owns vast stretches of farmland, it is also involved in the manufacture of inputs, including chemical pesticides used by large and small farmers alike. Companies like Dow Chemical sell chemicals such as DDT throughout the Third World, although they contravene safety standards in the developed countries. As a recent report commissioned by Oxfam put it, 'unless changes are made it may not be far from the truth to say that, rather than feeding the hungry, pesticides will be poisoning the hungry to feed the well-fed' (Bull 1982: 96).

The damaging effects of pesticide use are many. Pesticides not only kill crop pests, they also kill the natural enemies of target pests. They carry a considerable health risk to humans from contact with toxic sprays, and build resistance in some pest species. Finally, they contribute to harmful residues in food which persist even after food processing (Bull 1982).

The effects of pesticides are not distributed equally throughout the rural population of Third World countries. They fall particularly heavily on the poor. As the Oxfam report cited above expresses it, 'the poorest cultivators are the most likely to be using poorly maintained equipment and to lack the training and literacy which could safeguard their health' (Bull 1982: 80). The excessive dependence on pesticides imposes a burden on peasant farmers in the allocation of scarce resources, but the conditions under which they are 'competitive' are established by the multinational corporations. For farm labourers, such as cotton plantation workers in Central America, poisoning from pesticides is a daily event (ibid.: 78–80).

In recent years international agribusiness has spread to Africa, with similar effect. After reviewing the organization of agribusiness in Kenya and Tanzania and analysing the effect of agribusiness activities in coffee and sugar production, Dinham and Hines (1983) evaluate the contribution of agribusiness to Africa's food crisis. As their report makes clear, agribusiness companies have traditionally confined their attention to export cash crops for the high income markets of Western Europe and North America. However, such is Africa's food crisis, food production *per capita* having declined over the last two decades, that attention has now shifted to the domestic market for foodstuffs. African governments have encouraged agribusiness to produce for the domestic market because of the increasing cost of food imports. In 1981 African countries planned to import eighteen million tons of food, eight million tons of which could only be purchased if available at concessionary prices (Dinham and Hines 1983: 139).

The invitation that African governments have extended to agribusiness arises from two related factors. On the one hand there is little confidence in their own peasant farmers' ability to meet food shortfalls. On the other, the pressing cost of staple foods, notably grains, imposes an impossible burden on the less prosperous African economies. Large-scale, technically sophisticated projects are favoured by African countries because the technology they employ promises quick results. It is frequently the same technology as that employed by agribusiness in the developed countries. At the same time international lending agencies, such as the World Bank, are keen to provide funds for easily managed integrated projects. The alternative, a policy to secure food supplies through the increased participation of marginal peasant farmers in the market economy, is considered more difficult in management terms and more politically vulnerable. The interests of government and agribusiness coincide. As Dinham and Hines report, 'aid agencies effectively guarantee payments and therefore eliminate the financial risks to agribusiness' of involvement in under-capitalized African countries (ibid.: 144).

The benefits to be derived from agribusiness penetration of food-crop production are largely illusory. By turning their back on peasant production, governments have accelerated existing biases in favour of urban areas. In the field of cash-crop production African governments are relatively powerless in the face of protracted negotiation for international price support agreements and quota systems. Most of the marketing and processing of food is in the hands of large foreign companies such as Nestlé, General Foods, Unilever and Tate and Lyle. Where crops are processed and packaged in Africa, foreign exchange is required to pay for the foreign-produced inputs. In the case of Kenya, quoted by Dinham and Hines, Del Monte imported almost everything it needed before canned pineapples could be exported: 'The result is not only overdependence on foreign companies, but also a strong probability that more foreign exchange will be expended to pay for these capital-intensive developments than is received from the sale of canned pineapples' (1983: 158). International agribusiness is adept at using its power of persuasion, expressed increasingly through a 'consultancy' role, in helping to formulate African food policy. Such consultants are not disinterested. Their companies' financial interests are those of the parent corporation. Within Third World agriculture they seek high profits through the employment of cheap labour and the mobilization of capital assistance from governments and the national bourgeoisie. Besides the disappointments which agribusiness development brings, 'the main achievement . . . has been to provide, at cheap prices, a continuous supply of raw materials consumed in industrialised countries' (Dinham and Hines 1983: 160).

This brief examination of the relationship between agribusiness and food production has sought to identify the structural processes that underlie shifts in land use throughout the South. In Latin America the expansion of United States-owned agribusiness has been assisted by the failure in most countries to implement redistributive agrarian reforms, such as were advocated two decades ago in the CIDA studies (Barraclough 1973). Traditional landlordism has given way to industry-linked commercial farming, because the urban population has swollen without any real improvement in the economic and social position of the mass of peasant farmers and rural labourers. Even countries such as Peru, which have undertaken the reform of the estate system, in commercial coastal farming as well as the highlands, have conspicuously failed to extend the benefits of agrarian reform to the mass of peasant smallholdings.

In Africa, agricultural land use has been altered because of the scale of food deficits and the urgency of population pressure on food resources. Corporate farming, both private and state-organized, has opened the door to international agribusiness corporations. As we have seen, this has been at the cost to the natural environment and the livelihoods of most rural people. Land resources have been mortgaged to short-term commercial interests rather than developed in a sustainable way. Once again environmental poverty serves as a stimulus to increased economic dependence, rather than a signal that alternative development models need urgent consideration.

This chapter has considered natural resources and the use to which they are being put. Whether it is land, water or forest resources that are considered, the indications are that resource uses imply a concentration of control in fewer hands for short-term gain, at the expense of the longer-term benefit to the environment and the largely poor, rural populations, whose livelihoods depend upon better resource conservation. The next chapter considers the growth of environmental consciousness in the developed countries and the implications of this for the way in which 'development' is conceptualized.

3

Environmentalism and development

Earlier chapters have examined the limitations of political economy in providing an adequate theoretical understanding of environmental change, and the way in which the use that is made of natural resources seriously prejudices more equitable development policies. This chapter deepens this analysis by examining what is missing in the theoretical treatment of development and its practical implications for resource use. The evolution of an environmentalist perspective is identified in the concern for conservation and ecological balance in the developed countries. This concern has been expressed at the international level by environmental research programmes such as UNESCO's 'Man and the Biosphere' and the World Conservation Strategy, launched in 1971 and 1980 respectively. To what extent can the conservation approach advocated in industrialized societies, and given at least nominal support by many international development agencies, provide a framework for understanding environmental problems in the South? Is the urgency of the earth's resource problems reflected in a similarly urgent quest for an environmentalist perspective that is relevant to Third World conditions? In the last section of the chapter the environmentalist perspective of Rudolf Bahro, the principal theoretician of West Germany's Green Movement, is compared with that contained in the Brandt Report, in the light of these questions.

ENVIRONMENTALISM IN DEVELOPED COUNTRIES

Our perceptions of the environment have evolved with the development process. Environmentalism is an elusive concept which has spawned complex and different social movements. We shall begin by examining the environmental idea itself, and follow through the various components of this idea in western industrial societies.

Early expression of interest in the future of the natural environment was anti-urban and anti-industrial. In North America the transcendentalists, writers such as Thoreau, Whitman and Emerson, 'preached the notion of a bioethic, a sense of responsibility for the earth and a plea for a basic ecological understanding before tampering with its resources' (O'Riordan and Turner 1983: 3). They sought the defence of nature, particularly wilderness, from the ravages of civilization. In Europe, the antecedents of the environmentalists were principally in the early anarchist movement and among those socialists, like William Morris, who wanted to resurrect pre-industrial values in work and craftsmanship. Here the accent was on self-reliance and equality. This 'utopian' strand in environmentalism persists to the present day. Cotgrove distinguishes it from the more pragmatic school of thought which argues for a better relationship with nature within industrial society. The utopian stream of environmentalism, by contrast, begins with a 'radical rejection of the core values of industrial society, with its faith in economic growth and political solutions' (Cotgrove 1983: 19).

Much of the environmentalist message is concerned with finding new forms of co-existence with nature. Environmental fundamentalism argues that man's appropriation of nature needs careful justification:

> To the environmentalists, uncertainties about the precise effects dictate a stance of caution toward intervening with nature. But the position of some environmentalists goes beyond a concern for the possible negative effects upon people of altering the natural environment. Their fundamental premise is that nature should be left unaltered unless and until it can be shown that interference is truly necessary.
> (Tarris 1976: 57)

The view that nature exists *for* man is uncompromisingly challenged. Nature needs to be protected for its own sake, not merely to preserve its potential for man.

This concern with the stewardship of the natural environment has been married to the idea that human respect for nature is lost in the pursuit of material gain. Materialism, the production of goods from nature, represents an abdication of human responsibility for the natural world. It is not difficult to recognize the strength of ethical commitment in the environmentalist perspective, and these ethical concerns are not as recent as one might think.

What has given the debate about the quality of life an added urgency is the pace at which natural resources are being depleted and the environment polluted. It is this that has led some groups 'to use environmental dangers as levers to promote fundamental social change' (Cotgrove 1983: 19). At the same time, those who espouse the new 'philosophy of human conduct' which environmentalism implies (O'Riordan 1981: ix) also seek to practise it. This is important because, as will be argued later, one of radical environmentalism's principal weaknesses is the absence of a theory which explains how the new society is to be brought about. In the interim, heightened environmental consciousness dictates a search for less wasteful ways of using natural resources and a return to 'human-scale' technologies.

The ethical commitment in environmentalism has been buttressed by a number of important changes in the natural world which technology has precipitated. The first of these is the threat which is posed to the 'carrying capacity' of ecosystems by the increase in human population and the non-renewability of resource development. In an influential book, Barry Commoner expressed the dangers of this process in apocalyptic terms:

> Human beings have broken out of the circle of life, driven not by biological need, but by the social organization which they have devised to 'conquer' nature: means of gaining wealth which conflict with those which govern nature.   (Commoner 1972: 299)

A lack of respect for the environment has lost man his margin of freedom to proceed by trial and error (Dasmann 1975: 19). Although technology has enabled man to increase carrying capacity in ways that were previously unimaginable, 'ultimate limits remain' (ibid.: 36). Unless we can respect these ultimate limits our very survival is at stake.

Other threats posed to nature by man's rapaciousness are no less important. There is the 'biological magnification' argument, for example. This states that toxic substances deposited by man in nature are magnified by food chains. Environmental pollution is translated into threats to human nutrition (Dasmann 1975: 24–5). More dramatically, man is responsible for the survival of other species. Norman Myers, in a justly celebrated work, argues that in some parts of the planet the threat to the survival of the species posed by development has material consequences which we are only dimly aware of. Maintaining the 'gene pool' is necessary not merely for scientific or aesthetic purposes, but because with fewer genetic materials available to us the capacity of nature to adapt is seriously impaired (Myers 1979).

Another recent concern, which has given added impetus to the environmentalist position, is that represented by the 'limits to growth' thesis. Even before the industrialized countries were faced with economic recession, the continuing viability of the growth model had been questioned on other grounds (Meadows et al., 1972). The cost of making demands on a finite earth would be paid by future generations, to whom present human values might appear absurdly wasteful. The difficulty lay in reading the signals left by the biosphere before it was too late. As Eckholm has observed: 'The biosphere seldom presents human society with imperatives; rather we face choices about what sort of world we want to live in. Responses to environmental threats can be formulated only in relation to broader human goals' (Eckholm 1982: 209). Clearly ethical issues lie at the heart of environmentalism which 'by its very nature . . . challenges many of the motives, aspirations and achievements which support the contemporary world' (Newby 1980a: 105).

The different sources of inspiration for an environmentalist perspective have contributed to varied, often contradictory, movements. Some, like Stretton, argue that to be effective the environmental movement should 'be part of a programme of more general social change', and criticize the Left for its inability to recognize in the privatization of social life a challenge to broaden socialist concerns (1976: 4). Others, equally conscious of the way in which the environment is 'consumed', argue that 'positional goods', like the countryside, acquire value only when access to them is restricted (Hirsch 1976). Such a view challenges a fundamental assumption of social democracy: that it is the job of government to ensure a better distribution of goods, either by making them more available (in the case of consumer goods) or by improving access to them (in the case of public services).

Among the few sociologists to analyse the environmental movement is Cotgrove. His main concern has been to distinguish the environmentalist approach, manifested in the advice given to official bodies and the attempt to shift public opinion, from the more single-minded approaches to the environmental problem espoused by utopian groups. Cotgrove undertakes a sociological analysis of the environmentalist's blueprint for survival, in which we can perceive an image of the kind of society which is being advocated. He finds such blueprints contradictory and ill-defined (Cotgrove 1983). Although correctly identifying that 'what is generally missing is any account of how we get from here to there' (ibid.: 24), he does not pay much attention to the practical activity of utopian groups, which play an important part in maintaining credibility and channelling the energies of members. Activities like organic horticulture, handicrafts and experiments in communal living may seem remote from the new Jerusalem, but they are an essential element in establishing the idea that personal rewards do not depend upon financial or material gain.

Other analyses of environmentalism have concentrated on the view that different groups have taken of science. Sandbach distinguishes two types of environmentalism, one that is basically ecological and scientific, and a second that is more radical in inspiration. Proponents of the first view attempt 'to influence policy by presenting a valid, scientifically argued case, based upon ecology and systems analysis' (Sandbach 1980: 22). This group is often conservative in the sense that it believes existing environmental systems are viable, and thus legitimate. The second type of environmentalism is more anti-establishment, 'less concerned with environmental systems, but more with whether or not science and technology are compatible with humanistic principles' (ibid.: 23). According to Lowe and Worboys, advocates of the more radical persuasion argue that 'political differences are equally redundant, but this is because of the *imperatives* of man's ecological situation' (1980: 436). Sandbach probes further than most writers into the ideological inspiration for the radical varieties of environmentalism, and finds it in Habermas and Marcuse, both of whom look upon alienation and social control as products of science and technology. Both types of environmentalists are highly suspicious of political action, however much they might lean towards the Right and the Left. The popular ecology variety is the more positivist, arguing that value-free scientific analysis rests upon a political consensus. To the more conservative ecologists the environmental crisis is a crisis of science's authority in society. To the more radical environmentalist the crisis is one *within* science. For the radicals, science (as currently practised) is part of the *problem* not part of the solution. The search, however, will take us beyond the boundaries of conventional science and conventional technology. It will involve widening 'the terms of analysis, the range of alternatives, and the boundaries of the system to be analysed' (Brooks 1976: 128).

Serious problems remain for those who do not advocate an alternative society, but seek to 'shift the burden of proof as between the advocates of growth and the advocates of restraint' (ibid.: 128). The principal area of neglect has been that of the distributional consequences of conservation measures. Sandbach notes that the administrative costs of resource conservation and pollution control are borne by the public, rather than the companies that do the polluting. Better environmental standards are obtained through a tax on the public, of whom the poor are most likely to feel the extra cost (Sandbach 1980: 37). In this case environmental policies are regressive. The adversary procedure adopted in the United States, through which environmental safeguards are introduced as the result of pressure from the lobby, is particularly expensive. In addition, it provides a good example of the way those opposed to environmental protection can subvert opposition 'declaring themselves practising environmentalists, but insisting on the costs of excessive regulation and the intransigence of their opponents' (Wolfe 1980: 91).

As Newby acknowledges, the debate over environmentalism is a deeply political one, since it is concerned with the claims of individuals on society and the satisfaction of wants through non-market mechanisms (Newby 1980a). However, research into the activities of environmental groups rarely identifies distributive consequences. This is true for North America as well as the United Kingdom (Buttel 1979: 465). Where individuals or groups express an interest in conservation, this interest is usually accepted at face value, although as a recent study of farmers in East Anglia asserted, 'we may draw a distinction between what land-owners state as their motives for conserving the environment . . . and the objective consequences . . . with regard to their material and political interests' (Newby *et al.* 1978: 242).

Just as remarkable as the range of environmental concern, and the urgency with which it is expounded, is the search for a social theory which is both consistent with ecological principles and which could provide human agents with a way of averting ecocatastrophe. Most environmentalist writing places emphasis on the need for political decisions in laying the basis for sustainable development. However, there is considerable confusion over the likelihood, and efficacy, of better environmental policy. Unable to avoid the temptation to build 'the social factor' into their environmental advocacy, most authors nevertheless fail to identify both the *agency*, without which nothing can be achieved, and the *mechanism* through which environmentalist policies will be implemented.

Riddell's recent book is a case in point. The implications of not being sensitive to environmental issues are cogently expressed:

> growth in the original versions [of consumer society] was necessarily based, among other things, on inequality within and between nations. Who, then, can these poor nations now exploit for their own growth but themselves, creating in the process the self-same dividend society which independence from colonialism was to absorb.
>
> (Riddell 1981: xi)

Nevertheless 'ecodevelopment' is a normative concept, not an analytical one, in Riddell's usage. It is founded on an ideal of pantheism 'which is more resource-conscious, and neither atheistic (like Marxism) or theistic (like Christianity)' (ibid.: xiii). Underlying the case for 'ecodevelopment' is the personal conviction that 'human progress' is better served by 'soft change' than hard technology. He recognizes the need for a better allocative system based on an alternative mode of production, but gives no indication of the historical conditions under which such a mode might appear. The programmatic content in Riddell's analysis, for which he draws on Dickson's *Alternative Technology*, is attractive and persuasive (Riddell 1981; Dickson 1974). But we are no closer to an understanding of how such a programme can be introduced politically.

The search for a social theory which would ensure the adoption of an environmental perspective eludes other writers. It has been suggested that better conservation might begin by penalizing the groups that do the polluting (Fraser Darling 1970: 29). However, as we have seen, most legislative controls on pollution are much more modest, and depend upon the consent of the guilty party (Sandbach 1980). An awareness of environmental dangers also implies a willingness to forfeit real advances in income for rather less tangible environmental benefits (O'Riordan 1981: 309). The new environmental consciousness which might inform public debate is represented by 'life interests' rather than class interests (Bahro 1982a). Unlike the proletariat in the Marxist analysis, such interests cannot be contained in the womb of the old order.

Despite the need for concerted action human societies seldom restrict freedom for environmental motives. As we have seen, there are few imperatives to social action in the working of the biosphere, even if we ignore the warnings that exist. Most social organization is geared to improving access to goods and services, or ensuring that their 'collective consumption' provides industry with a contented labour force (Castells 1977). Except for short-term private gain, people show a marked reluctance to organize politically for environmental ends. Stretton's axiom, that 'people cannot change the way they use resources without changing their relations with each other', contains a basic truth which is none the less elusive (Stretton 1976: 3). The construction of more effective social institutions requires 'better means than exist today for classifying the realistic alternatives available, for establishing societal goals, and for achieving the alternatives that are most consistent with those goals' (Meadows *et al.* 1972). The search for a social theory which would enable environmentalism to gain political credibility promises to be a long one.

THE ENVIRONMENT IN DEVELOPING COUNTRIES

The environmentalism that has emerged in the developed, industrial countries has characteristics that cannot be extended to the Third World and might be considered ethnocentric. By way of illustration we can take the term 'countryside', a familiar category to people in the United Kingdom and continental Europe, but unknown outside these narrow geographical boundaries. The closest approximation to 'countryside' in Latin America − '*el campo*' − evokes hostility rather than pride in most urban people. The term does not stand for the rural idyll or pastoral plenty which exerts a hold on British sensibilities (Newby 1980b) but for poverty and repression. People seek to leave the countryside, rather than gain better access to it. The rural environment in Latin America is the location for two competitive social and economic systems: commercial farming (often large-scale) and subsistence agriculture. The rest is wilderness. The wilderness inhabits the minds of poets and thinkers, but does not occupy the recreational time of those with the resources to visit it. Middle-class recreation is spent at affluent watering-holes and seaside resorts, on old *haciendas* and new sports complexes. The countryside is for those who are poor or who can capitalize on the poverty of others to make money for themselves.

The contrast with industrial societies is obvious, and carries implications for the way the environment itself is conceptualized. In the developed countries the growth of agribusiness has led to increased vigilance over the *quality* of the countryside, since it is the countryside which is consumed through recreation and tourism. In most parts of the South no such case could be mounted by those who oppose agribusiness. The effects of agribusiness on the natural environment are often worse than in the developed countries, as we have seen, but agribusiness penetration is thought to have a 'positive' value, by contributing towards 'development'. Those whose delicately balanced agricultural systems are undermined by natural resource development are obstacles to modernization, people without a voice.

The very different content of the word 'environment' should make us wary of international comparisons based exclusively on European or North American experience. Dasmann, in an otherwise persuasive study, argues that:

> The conservation movement as a social force had its origins in the United States with a concern for the future of wild places and wild animal life. It now appears that it must make its final stand also in the United States. This country is in the strongest position to make the major changes that must come.
> (1975: 2)

Such a view, however nobly inspired, ignores the fact that in the less developed countries rural areas are dedicated to agricultural production rather than consumption by urban groups. Multiple land use is rare. In such areas environmental problems *are* development problems. The conditions under which environmentalism became established in North America and Europe do not exist. Food supply is often insecure even where food production is adequate, and population growth under highly inequitable land-tenure systems continues to exert pressure on food availabilities. In the developed countries the lower priority needs, such as freedom from pollution or planning blight, assume importance because higher priority needs, such as housing and food, have already been satisfied for majority groups. Indeed, the extent to which high priority needs are satisfied seriously prejudices the satisfaction of low priority needs. By contrast, in developing countries the higher priority needs retain their priority and constitute the battleground for environmental politics. The peasant movements that resist land engrossment by agribusiness corporations, and the urban squatters who seek titles for their homes, are the closest approximation to environmental action groups in the South.

In those countries which have achieved a significant degree of industrial growth there is abundant evidence that environmental activity follows class lines, dictated by the participation of different groups in the country's development model. Thus Sunkel locates environmental problems within a dependency framework, in which the economic development model provides the parameters:

> The surplus generated by the exploitation of nature allows an extremely favourable and pleasant artificial environment to be created for the middle and high income sectors, but for the broader sectors of the population the results are fairly precarious. This gives rise to a state of affairs in which the environmental concern of the affluent sectors rests on the quality of life, which is threatened by atmospheric pollution, noise, congested transport, etc., whereas the environmental concerns of the poor – water pollution, distance from places of work, precariousness and crowding of housing, etc. – threaten their very lives.
>
> (1980: 47)

The class basis of environmental action may lead to some unexpected political alliances in less developed countries. As Marshall Wolfe argues, 'encouraged by their employers [the workers] can . . . be expected to perceive environmental regulations as threats to their employment and their access to the consumer society' (1980: 88). The consumer society, which some have tired of in the North, represents an unattainable goal for many in the South. Without the material security that development has brought, market forces expose the poor to environmental decay and political impotence. Much of the development literature has demonstrated that even localized development processes are intimately linked to national and international economic exchanges. Contemporary conflicts over the environment in developing countries are part of the same process; their articulation by specific social classes part of the same contradictions.

In the developed countries the concern with the quality of life during the 1960s and 1970s has been compounded in the 1980s by severe economic recession. This has led to a radical re-examination of the meaning of work, and the recognition that informal labour processes are often similar in developed and developing countries (Redclift and Mingione 1984). Although capital may be restructured in the course of economic recession, the implications for the environment remain. As Habermas puts it:

> The possibilities of averting ecological damage are specific to individual systems, late capitalist societies have difficulty in obeying the imperatives of limiting growth without giving up their basic principle of organisation, because the transformation of spontaneous capital growth into qualitative growth demands planned production which is oriented towards use-values.   (1976: 371)

In this section we have examined the differences between environmental action in the developed countries and in the South. Before considering the new directions which radical environmentalism is taking, we must review the part played by international conservation in seeking to effect changes in the way development in the South is undertaken.

INTERNATIONAL CONSERVATION: THE ROAD FROM STOCKHOLM

There has been a discernible shift in the urgency given to international conservation efforts since the early 1970s. Over ten years ago, at a seminar convened by the United Nations, the tone was sanguine:

> As we have repeatedly stressed, the problems of environmental disruption are still a relatively small part of the development concern of the developing countries, and it may be premature for many of them to divert their administrative energies to the establishment of new institutions or machinery.   (UN 1972: 27)

This tone did not prevail, and largely as a result of the Stockholm Conference international conservation began to assume more importance. The new urgency with which environmental problems were raised was suggested by a shift in the environmental agenda from the concerns of developed countries (pollution and non-renewable fossil fuels) to those of natural resource degradation in the South (deforestation, desertification and the threat posed to irrigation systems). Immediately before the Stockholm meeting, in 1971, UNESCO had launched its 'Man and the Biosphere' programme, aimed at identifying environmental problem areas and developing interdisciplinary research methods for better environmental management. The research enterprise was 'to provide the kind of information that [could] be used to solve the problem at hand' (UNESCO 1982: 373).

Notwithstanding the 26 principal resolutions that were passed at the Stockholm meeting, and the 109 recommendations that received the assent of the participants, a retrospective review undertaken ten years later revealed the failure of international action on almost every count. Human population had increased in the decade by almost 800 million; the disparity between rich and poor nations had increased, too. The world's expenditure on arms had soared to over 500 billion United States dollars annually. The number and intensity of known toxins in the food chain had increased. The number of endangered species of plants and animals had also increased (Environmental Conservation 1982: 91). Superficially, at least, international conservation efforts had done little to combat the environmental crisis in the developing countries.

During the same decade environmental issues had assumed much more importance in the political agenda of developing countries. In 1972 many influential leaders in the South had taken the view that the protection of their environments constituted another attempt by the North to impose trade barriers, in the form of expensive pollution controls, on the South. Ten years later the leaders of the same countries, meeting under the auspices of the United Nations Environment Programme (UNEP) in Nairobi, 'expressed concern at the damage being done to their countries' environments, and specified the adverse effects this had on their development plans and on the condition of many of their people's lives' (Sandbrook 1982: 2–3). There was greater recognition that environmental problems in the South could only be solved through the concerted action of several countries. The most intractable, long-term problems called for global co-operation and the principal obstacles to this were political rather than technical (Global 2000 1982: 429).

The most telling diagnosis of the global environmental crisis was contained in the World Conservation Strategy, launched in 1980. The Strategy was essentially a diagnostic exercise and, as such, brought coherence to the debate about resource conservation. The relationship between ecosystems was clearly charted, and the threats to them set out in trenchant, readable prose. The approach forsook narrow geographical boundaries. The Strategy linked the fate of the 40 per cent of the world's population that inhabited lowland, mainly irrigated environments with that of the 10 per cent whose highland watershed systems fed lowland agriculture. Soil erosion and infertility, sedimentation and salinity were linked to over-grazing, deforestation and hillside flooding. They were interpreted as a direct result of the human pressure on land, exacerbated by poverty. The Strategy went further, identifying the development processes which were contributing to environmental degradation, notably the conversion of good cropland to ranching, the plunder of the world's forest resources by logging companies and the damage caused to lowland agriculture by excessive dependence on chemical fertilizers and insecticides. The three principal objectives of resource conservation were outlined: the maintenance of essential ecological processes and life support systems, the preservation of genetic diversity and the sustainable utilization of species and ecosystems. After reading the documentary evidence it was difficult to see why 'conservation and development [had] so seldom been combined that they often appeared – and [were] sometimes represented as being – incompatible' (WCS 1980). The case for conservation-minded development could hardly be better put.

On closer examination many of the assumptions behind the World Conservation Strategy can nevertheless be challenged. Sympathetic commentators have not always recognized these limitations, and have assumed that the negative responses to the Strategy by national governments are attributable to ignorance (Worthington 1982: 97). A less charitable explanation might be advanced. Despite its diagnostic value the World Conservation Strategy does not even begin to examine the social and political changes that would be necessary to meet conservation goals. It could be objected that such questions lie outside the remit and competence of those who drafted it. However, the absence of a discussion of ways and means of implementing policies, given the existing balance of social forces in the South, cannot be explained away so easily. As Brookfield has argued, 'to a great degree, the object of ecosystem study is to influence the decision-making process, but *the manner in which decisions are reached* is also of major importance to the study of ecosystem operation' (1982: 378). He might have added that the analysis of the decision-making process in environmental management is also important for the credibility of international conservation.

A comparison with the Brandt Commission Report, published at about the same time (1980), is instructive. Brandt acknowledged that basic development objectives were threatened by 'the irreversible destruction of the ecological systems of a number of poor countries' (Brandt 1980: 47). This process constituted a threat to world security, bringing in its train political instability and massive social problems (ibid.: 73). In similar vein the Second Report of the Brandt Commission referred to the continued and accelerating destruction of the developing countries' environment, which already assumed 'emergency proportions' (Brandt 1983: 126). Yet reading the World Conservation Strategy alongside Brandt one is left to speculate abstractly about the political conjunctures under which policies might be reversed.

The environmentalist perspective has staked out quite different territory. It is normal practice to assume that 'in the matter of the management of natural resources we are dealing with a politically-neutral subject' (Sandbrook 1982: 6). The supposed political neutrality of the approach confers on it a legitimacy that more normative approaches could not claim, but only at the cost of blunting its analytical weaponry. The positivism of much research on natural resources is at odds with the integrative and ethical bias that we have observed in the environmentalist perspective.

By way of illustration, we can take the claim that international conservation research is interdisciplinary and crosses the natural science/social science barrier. Brookfield reports that fewer than 5 per cent of the 884 field projects undertaken by the Man and the Biosphere programme 'are in any true sense interdisciplinary as between the natural and social sciences' (1982: 376). The bulk of projects are concerned with natural phenomena or the impact on natural phenomena of human situations. Thus the study of resource management by human groups when it does occur, falls far short of being the 'integrative' approach extolled in the international conservation journals (UNESCO 1982; Environmental Conservation 1982). In a vivid illustration of this point Elliott examines an attempt to bring together plantbreeders and community development workers in a new course of development studies. The plantbreeders, he reveals, sought to maximize output per unit of land, while the community developers sought to increase the output *per unit of resource available to poor people*. Such objectives are not easy to integrate. He concludes that it is not simply a question of sharing intellectual discourse, 'but also of the ideological underpinning of this discourse'. Different development disciplines, in the natural and social sciences, still find it difficult 'to think in the categories of environmental management' (Elliott 1982: 6).

Although an integrated environmentalist approach may still be elusive, the methodological appeal of conservation techniques is increasingly strong for policymakers. Environmental impact analysis is widely employed in the United States and has become an integral part of project appraisal as undertaken by the World Bank. A new breed of 'enlightened technocrat' has emerged from within the corpus of conservation professionals. Those who support this development note that 'because their analyses are backed up by indications of undesirable environmental damage and social distress, their views are gradually being heard more and more by those who count' (O'Riordan and Turner 1983: 12). Others are more sceptical:

the utility of such a tool [of analysis] as a method of selecting a specific solution for all parties to agree upon or at least to accept, is always dependent on a basic agreement among value perspectives.

(Tribe, Schelling and Voss 1976: xii)

As we have seen, in the absence of agreement about values, most environmental research proceeds by assuming that conflicts of values lie outside their terrain. Environmental research is conducted, as a consequence, as if it were unproblematical.

LEFT ENVIRONMENTALISM

This chapter has examined the growth of environmental consciousness in the developed countries, and compared this perspective and the social movements that have come to express it, with the very different problems facing the countries of the South. The positivist nature of much international environmental research was emphasized, and the contradiction between the orthodox version of conservation and the deeply ethical concerns of the environmental movement was outlined. Although the environmentalist perspective has not been fully assimilated within the political economy approach to development, it has none the less begun to exercise considerable influence on the thinking of the Left, especially on the Continent. In the concluding sections we look at the recent writing of Rudolph Bahro (1982a) the principal theoretician in the German Green Movement, and ask whether his writing suggests a closer fit between environmentalism and the political economy of underdevelopment.

Among the issues raised by Bahro the following deserve particular attention. First, he questions the relationship between personal lifestyles and political practice in the developed countries. Second, he argues that the ecological crisis dictates new political priorities for the Left. Third, and most provocatively, he outlines some revisions in Marxist thinking which the current crises in North and South make necessary. *Socialism and Survival* is a curious book, engaging the reader by the passion and conviction of its advocacy, while disappointing those who look to the Radical Greens for a thoroughly worked-out body of theory. As E. P. Thompson writes in the Preface, Bahro's vision 'does not refute the utopian mode'. If there were echoes of William Morris in Bahro's previous book, *The Alternative in Eastern Europe* (1978), there is more than a hint of Proudhon, Thoreau and the European anarchist tradition in the pages of *Socialism and Survival*.

Bahro is advocating what is sometimes called 'personal politics'. It is personal in the sense that the individual's behaviour is expected to be compatible with his wider ideological stance. Bahro seeks consistency between political positions and personal behaviour, including radically altered patterns of personal consumption and the commitment to feminist ideals. It is also 'personal' in a different sense, since altered consciousness is seen to rest on 'conversion' (his word) to a more ecological politics. As we shall see, this view departs radically from most Marxist thinking which views objective class interests as primary in determining the outcome of structural change (Bottomore 1982).

The liberating effect of the new ecological politics is attributed to the renunciation of the production/consumption ethos in advanced capitalism. Bahro's imagery is compelling on this point. What is required is not 'emancipation in economics [but] emancipation *from* economics' (ibid.: 33). The psychological underpinnings of capitalism have enabled the leisure time which technology affords us to be converted into yet another opportunity for the consumption of unnecessary goods. Inasmuch as capitalism has 'freed' the worker from the worst excesses of the labour process, it has sought to occupy his free time with 'compensatory needs' that bring neither happiness nor personal fulfilment. The contrived demand for ever more consumer goods pushes back the day when socialism can be 'afforded', and, by depleting the resources of poor people in the South, creates a more onerous and threatening form of exploitation than that which existed under nineteenth-century factory conditions in Europe. Alienated labour and 'the loss of emotional connection' between individuals in the North are mirrored in the South by increasing economic dependency and the loss of control over nature.

The second set of issues to which Bahro refers is concerned with the establishment of priorities on the European Left. In his view mankind's survival is under threat both from nuclear annihilation and the environmental crisis in the South. This dictates a new system of priorities, since socialism can never be achieved until the threat of nuclear war and eco-catastrophe have been averted. The immediate injustices of advanced capitalism are thus afforded a lower priority than the wider injustices implicit in the East–West, North–South conflicts:

> We can no longer behave as if the fate of us all depended on the outcome of domestic class struggles over wage levels, or on what party is dominant in the state. The tremendous contradiction on the North–South and East–West axes, which are inseparably bound together, overspill this context.   (Bahro 1982a: 20)

In Bahro's view our survival depends upon our ability to put existing development processes into reverse. In the North, society needs to be effectively *de*-industrialized, rather than *re*-industrialized, if only because the false competition between industrial nations provokes environmental depredation in the South. The first move should be nuclear disarmament, ending the artificial stimulus that the armament's industry produces, in both western capitalist, and eastern bloc, economies. Disarmament and a new world economic order are essential first steps towards resolving the ecological crisis.

Support for the present world economic order implies a deception, aimed at both ourselves and people in the South. We are deceived into believing 'that the commodity world that we find around is . . . a *necessary* condition of human existence' (ibid.: 27). Its defence lies in the constantly increasing nuclear arsenal at our governments' command. But even more objectionable is the deception we are practising on the South. Through complicity with capitalist industrial society we are following a model of development which the South cannot emulate. The expanded reproduction of capital requires the South's resources for *our* development; it has not the capacity to 'develop' the South in its own interest.

The third, and perhaps most provocative, element in Bahro's writing, is his critique of contemporary Marxist thinking and practice. In this critique he pulls together several strands in contemporary thought which, although at odds with the dominant ideology of capitalist society, are still insufficiently reflected in Marxism. To some extent they suggest, and Bahro supports this view explicitly, that Marxism's historical legacy has distorted its current promise (ibid.: 49).

Bahro's critique of contemporary Marxism is more thoroughgoing than he seems to realize. Few important ideas escape his revisionist attentions. The belief in the revolutionary potential of the proletariat is one example. Bahro feels this concept represents a considerable 'theoretical obstacle' to clear thinking, since the proletariat 'is not functioning in the way we were led to expect' (ibid.: 63). In his view the principal contradictions of capitalism are not observed in 'the institutionalised class struggle' within the developed countries, but in nuclear rearmament and the ecological crisis. The centre of gravity has shifted, as it were, from the workplace to the world stage.

The proletariat's role is more problematical than any of the classical Marxists suggested. As Bahro writes: 'The idea of the world-historic mission of the working class assumes that its class interests are directly identical not only with those of its nation as a whole, but also with those of all humanity' (ibid.: 64). He feels that the evidence for this proposition is limited. On the one hand it is not clear that, historically, any single, subordinated class 'has by itself anticipated the impending new order' (ibid.: 65). Should we make an exception for the proletariat? On the other hand, the orthodox Marxist conception of 'worker' is reductionist, denying a wider human status which, given the worker's reluctance to act like a revolutionary, many Marxists actually begrudge him (ibid.: 67). It is liberating the individual that provides the springboard to human liberation. The 'idea that it is enough to refer to the "class standpoint" in order to attain the level of a movement for general emancipation, no longer applies' (ibid.: 112).

The other essential strand in this re-evaluation of class analysis is Bahro's insistence that 'the alienated structure of people's needs' is inseparably linked to economic exploitation. Thus, 'it is only because capitalism exists . . . that the working people in the rich countries still have a relative need for rising incomes' (ibid.: 26). Although expressed as a solecism − if capitalism did *not* exist, neither would the working class − Bahro is giving expression to a deep-seated dissatisfaction with industrial capitalism. How much of labour under capitalism is socially useful? How can socialism replace expropriation with social appropriation, freeing the individual from the double-bind imposed by authoritarian structures and the creation of surplus value?

Reading Bahro one is struck by the fact that much contemporary sociology fails to make the necessary links between what is happening to Northern industrial society and development in the South. One wonders, specifically, whether the increased sophistication with which we handle the different dimensions of the international economy has not induced a blindness to shifting values and class aspirations in our own societies. Within the very broad brush-strokes of Bahro's writing can be discerned a new perspective, if not a new paradigm. Put simply, this is that the environmentalist consciousness developing in Europe, shorn of the parochialism evident in the American and British literatures, offers a more radical and enduring critique of underdevelopment than any other currently on offer.

From what has been written it is also clear that Bahro and the Greens hold a view of the 'mutual interest' between North and South that is radically different from that of much recent development theory, as expressed in reports like that of the Brandt Commission. The differences between these approaches can be expressed in diagrammatic form. Both positions draw attention to the impending crisis in the world economic system, but the analysis which each provides of this crisis and the prescriptions offered are so divergent that the Greens' analysis could be said to invert that of the Brandt Commission.

The 'North-South dialogue': two definitions of mutual interest

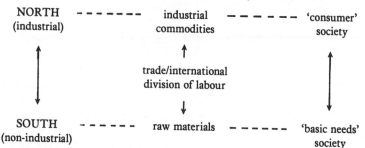

(1) *Brandt* (1980, 1983)

A The North is facing a crisis of under-production/consumption. This is the basis of the industrial recession. In both North and South there is a failure of demand, but for *different goods* (consumer society v. basic needs society).

B The solution for the North is to make the South richer through increased trade, bringing increased demand for industrial goods.

C Improved economic growth in the South, stimulated by trade, will help reduce poverty there, and improve provision of basic needs in the South.

(2) *Radical environmentalism* (Bahro 1982)

A The North is over-producing and over-consuming the *wrong* goods, particularly armaments. This is the basis of the ecological crisis.

B The solution for the North is to de-industrialize, reducing competition within the North to produce unnecessary consumer goods. This will also reduce inequality in the North.

C Reducing growth in the North would reduce demand for raw materials in the South, and help resource conservation there.

D The ecological crisis is a product of industrial growth in the North. Only ecological action towards alternative social provision can meet basic needs in the South (urban squatting, appropriate technology, preventive medicine).

CLOSING THE CIRCLE: THE PROBLEM OF HUMAN AGENCY

The perspective of the radical Greens departs from both orthodox Marxism and 'mainstream' environmentalism. They start with the premise that unless the environmental crisis is averted, no other important social goals will be achieved. What prevents necessary measures being taken to avert the crisis is not so much a lack of earnestness on the part of development agencies, as mainstream environmentalists suggest. Rather, it is in the interest of the industrial countries to maintain a North/South relationship, in which the progressive destruction of the environment is an inevitable consequence.

A decade ago the response of the Left to the environmentalist case was dismissive. Then it was possible to argue that the environmentalists' position was weak partly because it was universalistic. The destruction of the environment in the South was not total or irredeemable. Capitalism proceeded by uneven and combined development, depleting some resource systems more than others, and leaving in its wake important distributive consequences. *Some* people's resource base was destroyed to the benefit of others. The environmentalists, by refusing to characterize the process as capitalist, could offer no clues to the way it worked.

This accusation cannot be levelled at the radical Greens such as Bahro. They recognize that it is capitalist industrialization that poses the threat to peace and development. They also recognize that the costs of environmental destruction will not be equally borne. However, they see in capitalism no inbuilt capacity to resolve its own contradictions. Nor do they place their faith in the enlightenment of international development agencies, or interested individuals in the North to ensure human survival.

Bahro suggests that several processes provide grounds for optimism. First, the South's attempts to resist exploitation by making common commodity agreements, modelled on OPEC. Second, the pressure being mounted by trades unions in the North for a reduction in the working week and a better working environment. Third, the 'alternative' lifestyles based on co-operative arrangements for production and living which have blossomed in the developed countries since the 1960s. In a revealing passage he notes that 'It may well be that what is lacking above all are the forms of social organisation which these needs, often still embryonic, require for their further development' (Bahro 1982a: 113).

If we move, with Bahro, from 'class interests to life interests' we appear to be making a declaration of faith rather than a political judgement. Since class assumes so little importance in Bahro's writing, the burden for social and economic change falls, inexorably, on the individual. It is not 'human agency' as the expression of class interests but 'human agency' as *opposed* to class interests which Bahro is invoking. Although he appears to believe that Marxism has offered a workable analysis so far, today 'class membership . . . says next to nothing as to the actual role people play in a movement that transcends existing conditions altogether' (ibid.: 69).

The strengths of the Greens' position are also its weaknesses. First, their argument rests on personal convictions about survival that not everybody shares, and the *urgency* of which can be challenged. Second, it is unclear how consciousness of the need to resolve the ecological crisis will lead to action to solve it. By exorcizing economic determinism so completely from their Marxism, Bahro and his comrades can be charged with depriving the Greens' arguments of theoretical content.

At the same time, the radical Greens do present a challenge to both Marxist and environmentalist orthodoxies. In seeking to revert our attention to basic needs, rather than contrived consumption, in seeking to revise domestic priorities in the light of the global resource crisis, the radical Greens invoke the experience of the South. It is in this sense that Bahro and the radical Greens provide a challenge to those who, having declared an interest in the environment, fail to see it adequately reflected in Marxism. We shall return to these wider issues again in Chapter 7, where the ideological content of environmentalism and development is elaborated upon. In the next two chapters we take a closer look at the 'basic needs' society that exists in the South, beginning with an examination of the relationship between rural poverty and the physical environment.

4

Rural poverty and the environment

The previous chapter discussed the fact that the environmentalist perspective has been developed within a geographical and cultural setting, that of the northern industrialized countries, which is radically different from that of the South. At the level of international policy it was noted that an interest in conservation was rarely linked to demands for structural change in the international economy, and frequently ignored the political interests in resource development. In this chapter the structural causes of poverty in the South and their effects on the environment are explored in more detail. Poor environments are identified as areas in which structural processes of underdevelopment have had specific effects. The realization that poverty is often responsible for environmental depredation has been growing in recent years (Eckholm 1976, 1982). Nevertheless, poverty is still introduced as a *deus ex machina*, to explain environmental problems. The argument developed in this chapter is that poverty is structurally determined, that it reduces poor people's command over their own livelihoods and frequently contributes to political and social movements designed to redress growing inequalities. Without denying the importance of contingent factors, such as soil quality, in the acceleration of environmental distress (Blaikie 1981: 3), it is suggested that environmental poverty should not be disassociated from underlying structural conditions. The distribution of resources, especially land, is critical in determining the scale and incidence of poverty which, by pressing further on resource endowments, threatens to upset the ecological processes on which the societies of the South depend.

STRUCTURAL LINKAGES BETWEEN POVERTY AND THE ENVIRONMENT

Rural poverty is usually either explained in terms of socio-economic factors; that is, regarded as structurally induced, or it is looked upon as the outcome of impoverished natural resources. Both explanations contain elements of truth, but these elements need to be better integrated if we are to grasp the importance of the *relationship* between poverty and the environment. As Chambers has observed:

> Rural poverty is variously and to varying degrees attributed to a continuing condition of underdevelopment; to an active process of underdevelopment and the extraction of surplus through colonialism, neo-colonialism and the forces of capitalism and unequal exchange; to ill-health and poor nutrition; to war; to natural disasters; to famines; to population growth and its pressure on resources; to degradation of the environment; to the impact of inappropriate capital-intensive technology and the failure of government services to provide for basic needs.
>
> (1981: 1)

In practice the differences in approach reflect two clearly distinguishable perspectives: one which concentrates on underlying *causes* and attributes the conditions of poverty to other dependent variables; and the perspective which, although recognizing underdevelopment, is more concerned with the *effect* of poverty. An example of the former approach, representing most Marxist and neo-Marxist writing, is de Janvry (1981). In setting out his concept of 'structural dualism' de Janvry explicitly addresses what has been termed the 'logic' of poverty (Mitchell 1981). He writes:

> It is the extended period of primitive accumulation, in which a surplus is extracted from the traditional sector via the labour and wage-foods markets and in which the traditional sector gradually decomposes while sustaining rapid accumulation in the modern sector, that can be properly labelled the development of underdevelopment.
>
> (de Janvry 1981: 37)

For de Janvry underdevelopment and poverty are necessarily, and logically, connected. Any attempt to disconnect them is intellectually flawed.

Perhaps the most determined attempt to offer a theory of specific forms of poverty in the rural environment is that of Henry Bernstein in his discussion of the 'simple reproduction squeeze'. The situation Bernstein is describing is one in which land and labour have been exhausted using the existing techniques of cultivation, and market forces dictate the introduction of new means of ensuring that surplus is appropriated from peasant producers. These new means of production (seeds, tools, fertilizers, insecticides, etc.) prove a burden for the poor farmer, his returns to labour do not increase proportionate to his investments, and the terms of exchange for his saleable commodities deteriorate (Bernstein 1979: 427).

Increased commodity production is thus a vital factor in physical survival, undermining the peasant farmer's system of production, and ensuring ecological imbalance:

> As much of peasant production in Africa is fuelled by human energy (this is particularly true of Tanzania where hoe cultivation is the most widespread form), and as techniques of land use in many cases exhaust the soil after a certain period (the traditional solution – that of various rotational and fallow patterns of land use – being increasingly inhibited as commoditisation develops), the intensification of production occurs. This involves a greater expenditure of labour-time on poorer or more distant soils to produce the same output of crops, thereby increasing the costs of production and reducing the returns to labour.
>
> (Bernstein 1979: 427–8)

In Bernstein's view 'the low level of development of the productive forces in peasant agriculture' makes such producers more vulnerable to market forces, rather than inured to them.

Bernstein depicts a situation in which the real incomes of peasant farmers are falling in relative terms. In order to compensate for declining living standards relative to other groups, they have recourse to the natural environment. The process of environmental depredation is accelerated as a consequence. This is what Blaikie has in mind when he writes that:

> *under certain defined circumstances*, surpluses are extracted from cultivators who then in turn are forced to extract 'surpluses' . . . from the environment (stored-up fertility of the soil, forest resources, long-evolved and productive pastures, and so on) which in time and *under certain circumstances* lead to degradation and/or soil erosion.
>
> (1981: 21; my italics)

Blaikie introduces these observations in the context of a discussion about soil erosion. In this case the environmental effect is clearly specified. What remains problematical is the role of 'surplus' appropriation in its explanation. It could be argued that when the resource base becomes unsustainable, which it is at these levels of energy transfer, the viability of subsistence agriculture itself is put in jeopardy. The natural environment cannot 'replace' what the peasant farmer or pastoralist loses through market forces.

Clearly, not all structurally-induced environmental poverty leads to so intractable an outcome. Even absolute falls in real income might force peasants or pastoralists into various forms of commercial production without bringing imminent environmental collapse. Indeed, the 'externalities' generated through this process may be borne by other groups. Whether or not the peasant or pastoralist can, by these means, narrow the gap between his real income and that of other groups will, again, depend on specific circumstances. Considering the variety of possible, and actual, outcomes, it is important to distinguish between the environmental effects of structural processes and the likelihood that development will no longer be sustainable. Such an outcome is increasingly likely, but not logically necessary.

A quite different perspective on environmental poverty concentrates on its effects rather than its causes. True to its Keynesian antecedents, this view departs from the assumption that poverty is an inevitable consequence of development. One expression of this perspective is that of the International Labour Office (ILO). Like most international agencies the ILO is less interested in the theoretical diagnosis of causes than in suggesting policy prescriptions. Poverty is the designated 'problem' rather than 'underdevelopment'. Kitching summarizes this view as follows:

> Put simply, the ILO saw the problem of poverty as essentially an employment problem . . . because the bulk of poor people in the Third World could not find uses for their labour which were significant enough or remunerative enough to provide them with a minimum standard of living.
> (1982: 70–1)

The problem for the poor is that they are powerless to effect a change in the distribution of income, without which development is impossible. Sen perceived this in asserting that they are the victims of a 'tradition of thinking in terms of what *exists* rather than in terms of who can *command* what' (1981: 8). He points out that famines have often occurred in regions where food supply is normal and, equally significantly, rural poverty has been reduced in some countries, such as China, despite low agricultural growth. His analysis questions the assumption that it is population pressure on food supply that leads to rural poverty. If some groups become richer and exert more pressure on food supply, then the poor's command over food, which he terms their 'exchange entitlement', will be worse. Similarly, worsening employment possibilities can lead to worsening exchange entitlements. Sen's analysis applies equally to urban and rural groups, since what distinguishes the poor's position in society is not how they gain their income but how they spend it. What interests him is the way in which the allocation of 'bundles' of commodities corresponds neither to biological nor psychological needs, still less the abundance of goods being supplied (ibid.: 161). His work is an important contribution to a better understanding of the cycle of deprivation in which the poor are trapped.

These diverse approaches to poverty, illustrated by Bernstein's analysis of rural production and Sen's treatment of both urban and rural consumption, are structural in orientation. That is, they seek to explain poverty in terms of the way the market allocates income and goods. The rest of this chapter analyses the relationship between structural processes and the natural environment in specific rural areas of the Third World. Access to land and its distribution are identified as critical in determining how poor rural people have recourse to their environments. However, this does not enable us to read off the environmental consequences of development from a knowledge of land tenure. Reduced access to land can take the form of rural proletarianization, urban migration or land fragmentation. Moreover, the effects of land distribution on rural poverty need to be considered together with the effect of population increase on natural resources, as the discussion of Bangladesh illustrates. Most important of all, it is the relative position of groups of producers and consumers, dictated by the terms of trade that operate intersectorally and between different types of agricultural production, which determines the environmental outcomes of rural poverty.

RURAL POVERTY AND THE ENVIRONMENT IN AFRICA

Pre-colonial African society was organized on the basis of tribal or kinship rights. Land was rarely sold. Since the specialization of labour institutions was relatively undeveloped, technology simple, and dependence on the market confined to a few crops, the principal determinant of crop production and animal husbandry was the physical environment. Social relations involved obligatory gift-giving and receiving, in which resource use was based on ritual observance and tradition. The exchange of labour services played a large part in helping to guarantee the security of livelihoods. Access to land was a socially structured right, determined by the individual household's position within the tribal political structure. Few people were denied this right altogether (Cliffe 1982).

The penetration of capitalist relations of production came relatively late in Africa; some time had elapsed, indeed, since most Latin American states had received their political independence. The faith of early explorers like Livingstone that the abolition of the slave trade would pave the way for increased commodity production and exchange was borne out by history, although some decades later.

African societies possessed two features of value to capitalist penetration: a surplus productive capacity in land and labour time (Arrighi and Saul 1968). Their economies were structured around present consumption needs and largely unproductive accumulation. Such activities strengthened social cohesion, and to be successful capitalist development had to provide incentives for the use of surplus productive capacity. The continuing importance of this process, in the form of accelerated commoditization, is described by Bernstein (1979). The division of much of Africa into either 'settler' or 'plantation' societies testifies to the variety of forms of labour exaction and land use deployed in capitalist expansion, as well as the diversity of indigenous practices.

Participation in the growing capitalist economy was dictated by two factors: whether centres of labour demand, such as mines or plantations, existed, and whether local conditions favoured the production and marketing of agricultural crops (Saul and Woods 1971). In contrast to the situation in most parts of Asia, African peasantries were often 'labour exporting', enabling the subsistence base to survive (especially when it was the province of women) and releasing adult males from under-employment in traditional agriculture. Most indigenous crops were not those consumed on the international market, unlike the situation in Latin America where such crops (potatoes, tomatoes, beans and maize) became important food crops in the metropolitan states.

In many parts of Africa today aggregate statistics on land distribution provide few clues to the loci of power in rural society, precisely because they do not enable us to distinguish between communal systems of land-holding and the individualization of crop production that has accompanied the restructuring of capital in agriculture. In many parts of Africa the privatization of land and the role of merchant capital in landowner-ship are well developed (Shepherd 1981). Agribusiness is also increasingly important, as we saw in Chapter 3. Recently, the direct control over land that is exercised by capital has increased, serving to intensify class conflict and inequality during the last twenty years or so (Williams and Allen 1981; Cliffe 1982).

A superficial treatment of environmental change in Africa involves few references to structural underdevelopment, although such processes underpin the 'food crises' which have bedevilled large expanses of the continent for several decades. An example of a region in which environmental degeneration has been particularly rapid is the Sahel. On close examination many of the problems associated with resource use in the Sahel, and the cycle of drought and famine which have become synonymous with the region, can be attributed to underlying structural processes. The Sahel provides a vivid illustration of the danger in assuming that the specificity of environmental poverty reduces the explanatory role of structural analysis.

The Sahel covers six West African countries: Mauritania, Senegal, Mali, Upper Volta, Niger and Chad, with a combined population in

1974 of almost twenty-five million. The population most affected by the drought between 1969–74 was smaller, perhaps five or six million. About half of these people were nomads, eking out a vulnerable existence to the north of the settled savannah of West Africa. The other half was made up of marginal agriculturalists, many of whom had traditionally developed symbiotic relations with the herdsmen and their families.

Contrary to widespread belief, periods of extended drought are not common in the dry Sahel. There have been only three such periods since the turn of the century. During this century, however, the ecological vulnerability of the region has increased enormously. This has been due to a number of forces which have together compounded the effects of over-grazing on an already poor natural environment. During 'good' years when rainfall meets expectations, nomadic pastoralists increase their livestock to the point where it exceeds the carrying capacity of the environment. A sudden reversal can then throw this delicate ecological system into crisis. As Eckholm writes:

> Over and over again droughts are perceived as unexpected natural disasters just like tornadoes or earthquakes; the real calamity arises from the failure of societies to mould their habits to fit environmental reality. Human cultural patterns in the desert must be reshaped to survive the driest years, not to push the land to its limits in years of favourable rainfall.
>
> (1976: 67)

The over-grazing of semi-arid areas, like the Sahel, is linked to the analogous process through which more land is brought into arable cultivation. Both are responses to increased numbers of people, and the pastoralists are usually heavily dependent on the peasant farmer for obtaining cheap vegetable protein. The pastoralist's dependence on selling livestock makes him peculiarly vulnerable to market fluctuations. His structural position is more like that of the cash-crop farmer than the subsistence peasant, and he is similarly affected by a reduced command over food resources during famines. According to Sen:

> Compared with the farmer or the pastoralist who lives on what he grows and is thus vulnerable only to variations of his own output . . . the grower of cash crops, or the pastoralist heavily dependent on selling animal products, is vulnerable both to output fluctuations and to shifts in marketability of commodities and in exchange rates.
>
> (1981: 126)

It is thus impossible to separate the ecological processes that determined the strategies of the nomads and poor farmers of the Sahel from the political and economic conditions of the region. Deforestation, intensive agriculture and over-grazing were all responses to reduced environmental flexibility. The growth of commercial farming, especially cash-cropping, had reduced the mutual benefits to both pastoralists and peasant farmers. New crops such as cotton were harvested later than traditional food crops and dictated a different seasonal rhythm (Norton 1976: 260). Before the 'push' towards commercial farming much of the dry Sahel had resembled 'open-field' agriculture in rural England, the animals grazing on the post-harvest stubble and fertilizing the fields by providing dung. Commercial farming not only displaced the pastoralists from their land; it undermined their symbiotic relationship with food-producing peasant farmers.

The strategies adopted by pastoralists in the Sahel during 'good' years, together with the spread of modern medicines and better livestock disease-control, may well have 'encourage[d] ever larger populations of humans and livestock' (Eckholm 1976: 68). But these strategies were undertaken within a rapidly changing context. Capital intensive farming 'may have opened up new economic opportunities, [but] it has also tended to increase the vulnerability of the Sahel population' (Sen 1981: 127). The increasing dependence on markets for meeting food requirements has meant that, together with ecological imbalance and climatic variability, the region's population has been exposed to both situational and structural resource pressures. The individual pastoralist and agriculturalist resolves his basic dilemma by resorting to strategies which seriously restrict the environment's capacity to adjust, such as investing capital in more livestock or taking marginal fields into pro-duction. However, these strategies are inevitable given the structural conditions within which the population is forced to exist.

To underline this point we need only look at the way in which food supplies were distributed during the Sahelian drought. During the period 1968–72 there was a decline in overall food supply within the region. Nevertheless, various sources concur that the *per capita* supply of cereals still comfortably exceeded the FAO/WHO recommended mini-mum food intake (Marnham 1977; Lappé and Collins 1977, 1978; Lofchie 1975). More importantly, 'there is clear evidence that dramatic shifts in the distribution of purchasing power were taking place in the drought years in the Sahelian countries, mainly between the dry Sahel regions in these countries and the rest of the regions' (Sen 1981: 119). Food went with purchasing power. UNEP concluded that 'the drought in the Sahel would not have resulted in 100,000 deaths if priority had not been so clearly given to supplying the coastal towns with meat rather than improving the herder's living conditions' (UNEP 1981: 32). Government policies in the Sahelian countries also reflected urban and class biases that increased the pastoralists' and marginal farmers' vulnerability. The burden of taxation falls particularly hard on the poor, and the need to pay taxes in monetary terms helps explain the Sahelian farmers' shift from food to cash crops. There is also some evidence that the pastoralists who headed southwards during the drought were discriminated against by the governments of the region (Sheets and Morris 1976). The official preference for commercial agriculture, which would require vast petroleum imports to make up fertilizer requirements, is well documented (UNEP 1981: 16). What has received less attention is the systematic neglect of agricultural research (livestock and arable farming) geared to small farmers in arid and semi-arid regions (Wellhausen 1976). As Sen writes, 'since the source of the problem (in regions like the Sahel) is variability rather than a secular decline, it is tempting to think in terms of insurance arrangements' (1981: 128). For too long international agencies and government élites conspired in their neglect of strategies to reduce resource vulnerability in the region.

Some aspects of the Sahelian famine and longer-rooted poverty are peculiar to the region. Many other aspects are shared with other semi-arid environments. What is incontrovertible is that the structural processes at work in the region over a long period, particularly the growth of large-scale commercial agriculture, forced more of the rural population to make excessive demands of the natural resource base. At the same time distributive mechanisms were reducing the effective demand of the poor for food supplies. The environmental crisis, when it came, was not restricted to those who were producing food commodities, nor those who needed to buy them. It was a product of vulnerable production practices, inadequate effective demand and the complicity of those who benefited from a 'modernization' model of development. The 'closing circle' was pulled a little tighter as a result.

RURAL POVERTY AND THE ENVIRONMENT IN LATIN AMERICA

The ownership and distribution of land has always been highly contested in Latin America. Not because land is not available. The evidence suggests that additional land of arable potential exists throughout Latin America, particularly tropical zones in Mexico, Central America and Brazil (Posner and McPherson 1981; Kirpich 1979). The problem is that the control of land, once vested in a small class of landowners, has increasingly passed to corporate capital and governments representing the interests of international agribusiness. The political power of these classes depends upon maintaining the existing pattern of highly unequal land distribution and land uses.

The colonization of Latin America was undertaken by urban adventurers, for whom the principal economic activity was the mining of precious metals. Agriculture was a secondary activity, initially geared to the needs of the mining economy. The system through which large landed estates controlled labour, known as the *hacienda* system, grew out of the Conquistadors' need to draw upon indigenous labour power, particularly in those highly populated regions such as the Andes where a sizeable indigenous population remained. Under the original *encomienda* system, the control of land was only one of a number of mechanisms for ensuring the landlord's control of the labour force and the exaction of rent. As commercial agriculture developed and urban centres grew, the control of land sometimes became an objective in itself. In the evolution of the *hacienda* (estate), an institution with multiple functions providing patronage and some degree of social protection to the dependent labour force, the terms on which labour was employed varied widely. In different historical periods and under distinct geographical conditions, labour was attracted to the estate by the offer of a plot of land or retained through the threat of coercion. Off the estate peasant holdings provided an external labour reserve. The conditions governing the labour process were thus determined by the landlord's capacity to extract rent from his estate either in the form of labour or in kind. In neoclassical terms, the landlord's near-monopoly of land in a given locality provided him with an oligopsonistic control over the labour market (Griffin 1976).

If rent took the form of labour payments, these could sometimes be commuted into payments in kind or in cash. The landlord took a commercial interest in his estate, but was rarely involved in direct production. The capital generated in the rural economy was invested in the city rather than in agriculture. In plantation economies it was often exported. Frank was correct in observing that, prior to industrialization, the urban and rural bourgeoisie was often indistinguishable, even if he was wrong to assume that integration with capitalist markets implied a capitalist mode of production (Frank 1969; Laclau 1971).

In some parts of Latin America the growth of towns became linked, by the beginning of the twentieth century, with a marked degree of industrialization (Furtado 1970). However, food crops continued to be grown largely by the petty-commodity producing sector. Operating along parallel lines, the large estates had provided export earnings to finance the early stages of industrialization. The difficulties experienced in breaking free from the existing international division of labour persuaded some economists, working for the United Nations Economic Commission for Latin America (ECLA), to press for a deliberate policy of import substitution (Booth 1975).

The rethinking of trade theory, together with mounting disaffection in rural areas and the example of socialist Cuba, led to a new definition of Latin America's development problem. By the 1960s land distribution was identified as the heart of the problem. Without a major redistribution of land, it was predicted, the internal market for industrial products would remain small and rural discontent would rise. Rapid urbanization, which was compelling migrants into the 'marginal' zones of large cities, could only be stemmed by addressing rural problems. Empirical evidence for the wastefulness of the existing *latifundia/minifundia* system, low productivity of land on the estates and of labour on peasant holdings, was provided by the reports of the Interamerican Committee for Agricultural Development (CIDA) throughout this period. These studies fuelled the drive for a reform of land tenure throughout Latin America. Increases in agricultural productivity, ran the argument, depended on bringing unproductive land into cultivation, if necessary through the parcelization of estates. Tenants would be able to gain better access to modern inputs, such as fertilizers and credit, by being given titles to the land they worked (Barraclough 1973; Barraclough and Domike 1970). Land, rather than capital or labour, was looked upon as the critical element in rural development.

The political repercussions of this ideological strife were not as anticipated by most liberals. Although legislation evoked the 'social functions of property' in criticism of negligent landlordism, little land was transferred directly from landlords to individual peasant households during the 1970s. Some peasant farmers received land titles for the first time, others were 'assisted' in colonization attempts that were usually ill-planned and expensive (Delavaud 1980; Revel-Mouroz 1980; Barbira-Scazzochio 1980). In Peru, estates formerly owned by landlords were managed by the state, with nominal control being exercised by the workers (Guillet 1979, Long and Roberts 1979). Most countries studiously avoided lending assistance to the poorest peasant families and, particularly, landless agricultural labourers.

Indeed, one of the most important net effects of Latin American land reform has probably been an increase in landlessness. Agrarian reform, or the threat of it, stimulated private land sales and helped ensure that landlords divested themselves of their poorest land (Preston and Redclift 1980). Most landlords could be relied upon to modernize the land they retained with the incentive of generous government assistance. Others left for the towns where, in the absence of equitable public marketing systems and credit facilities, they controlled these commercial functions. Where rights were granted to groups of peasant families, it was impossible to ensure that they were enforced.

The diagnosis provided by CIDA, and taken up by various Latin American governments, was faulty. Inequitable systems of land tenure were the outcome of class interests and would remain so, unless equal attention was paid to changes in capital accumulation and its implications for the rural labour process. Some agrarian reform legislation actually facilitated the growth of large-scale agribusiness, enabling landlords to enter into economic alliances with the state or transnational corporations (Burbach and Flynn 1980). The demand for seasonal labour increased, often replacing the traditional labour institutions associated with the state system. This new form of rural proletarianization was linked with temporary wage-workers, the *boias-frias* (D'Incao e Mello 1976). Much of the Latin American countryside was populated by resource-poor peasants, seasonal migrants to areas of capitalist farming, working eroded land without any form of technical assistance (Goodman and Redclift 1981; de Janvry 1981). Finally, the natural resources that peasant communities held in common, such as woodland and common grazing, were subjected to systematic private exploitation or threatened by environmental depredation through over-use. In some cases the ownership and control of land had changed hands, but in most cases land concentration and landlessness had increased.

The exactions of a *rentier* class and the opposition mounted by peasant farmers in Latin America are demonstrated in the social conflicts that have provided a constant theme in Andean history and ethnography. The Andean region, as we have seen, was one of dense indigenous population. It included several distinct ecological zones, determined partly by altitude (Preston 1980: 8). At the same time the links between these regional ecological systems were important. They existed prior to capitalist penetration in the Inca empire, but assumed more importance once capitalism 'like a seamless web' had served to 'integrate rather than separate areas and groups with widely varying institutional structures' (Lehmann 1982: 1). In a recent edited collection Lehmann regards ecology in the Andes as a 'conditioning' rather than a determining factor in the way social institutions developed. The effect of population pressure on resources did not reduce inequality between peasant households. In effect, richer families used their wealth to acquire more or better access to natural resources, both communally and privately owned. Lehmann notes that:

such cases – which are the rule rather than the exception – show that abuse of power and a deviation from the 'original purpose' of the *comunidad* are inherent features of an institution established for tributary purposes, on the basis that some members of the *comunidad* are superior in status to others.   (1982: 25)

It is a well-attested observation that social institutions designed for one purpose, such as the 'community' in pre-Columbian South America, carry cultural implications beyond the historical context of their formation.

Control over resources in the Andes was determined by the prevailing systems of land tenure, reflecting established and emerging class interests. As we have seen, the dominant land-tenure system, bequeathed by the Spanish but modified throughout the nineteenth century to reflect the importance of the internal market, was that of the *hacienda*. In the Andes the dependent population that worked for the landlord (*hacendado*) was made up of the indigenous population, which had largely been exterminated in lowland areas. In the highlands the Inca civilization had been destroyed, but institutions like the *comunidad* and its associated farming practices, such as land-terracing, survived. The landlord worked his estate extensively, usually rearing cattle and sheep, so his labour requirements were not great. The shortage of land off the estate, and its poor quality, enabled the landlord to attract or coerce labour onto the estate without much difficulty. Most dependents were given the usufruct to a plot of land in return for labour services, or a share of the product to the landlord.

The penetration of capitalist production and marketing relations into the Andean highlands served to alter these social relationships in a number of ways. Occasionally, as in the La Convención Valley near Cuzco, the peasant farmers were able to improve their market position and, ultimately, gain a measure of political independence from the landlord (Hobsbawm 1969). But landlords' attempts to expel labour-tenants and introduce wage-labour, were more common, and violently resisted by the indigenous population (Martinez Alier 1977: 14). Frequently, the effects of capital penetration have been to increase social differentiation within communities:

> some villagers have become less concerned with the opportunities available in pastoral farming and more oriented towards outside possibilities. Hence, communities are divided between locally and extra-locally oriented members, which makes it difficult for them to identify common economic interests.   (Long 1977: 179)

The commitment to laudable development objectives and their own political survival dictated that the ruling class showed some interest in land reform. This was

> conceived in terms of juridical changes in the status of small producers, offering titles to tenant farmers, and thus enabling them to

obtain agricultural credit. The traditional highland *hacienda* was expected to be transformed into a modern capitalist enterprise once incentives existed for landowners. These incentives were to be provided by opening up their land to the market. Once this was effected they would cease to be *rentiers* and would be transformed into modern entrepreneurs.

(Goodman and Redclift 1981: 112)

Agricultural modernization was seen by some groups as both the goal of agrarian reform and the means of avoiding a radical redistribution of resources, including land.

During the last two decades the Andean countries have been living with the consequences of this ambiguity. In those countries which have carried out agrarian reforms designed to harness rural surpluses for industrialization, and to assist the development of a new commercial farming class (notably Chile and Peru), agrarian reform policies have effectively ignored the needs of the resource-poor peasant farmers. Without access to more land, credit or technical assistance, marginal farmers are pushed back onto their limited resource base at great environmental cost. Soil erosion and deforestation are the inevitable consequences of poverty among such producers.

In other countries the rural poor have fared no better. Despite superficial access to power since 1952 in Bolivia, and the recent return of civilian government in Ecuador, the mass of the Andean population has derived few tangible benefits from agrarian reform. Landlords have sought to open up a land market, ridding themselves of unproductive land and concentrating resources in those parts of their estates with commercial potential. In other cases, such as the Cajamarca Valley in Peru and highland Ecuador, multinationals have stimulated the milk economy by encouraging the vertical integration of simple commodity production (Rainbird 1981; Archetti 1977). The most common phenomena, observed throughout the Andes, is the continued reproduction of very small holdings, as peasant plots become further sub-divided and poor families receive land titles to miniscule plots (Preston and Redclift 1980; Rusque 1982).

The Andes illustrates the effect of the capitalist penetration of agriculture, both through agrarian reform legislation and its avoidance. What distinguishes the new agrarian structure is not so much the differences between the 'reformed' and 'unreformed' sectors as the increased vulnerability of peasant farmers, for whom the resource base is inadequate. Their response to the resource crisis is either to vote with their feet, by moving seasonally, if not permanently, to urban areas or tropical colonization zones, or to confront the situation through political rebellion. During the 1970s the latter course has met with increasing repression, often from the state rather than private landlords acting individually. The full extent of environmental pressure on the marginal farmer is thus impossible to measure, since social discontent has been relieved by migration from the sierra. The maintenance of a precarious livelihood, through supplementing cash income from work in the casual labour market of the towns with the minimum sustenance afforded by the family plot, has served to disguise the extent of ecological imbalance in the highland region.

RURAL POVERTY AND THE ENVIRONMENT IN BANGLADESH

In the previous sections we discussed poverty in Africa and in Latin America. We noted that the Sahel was a resource-poor region made poorer by the pressures on its carrying-capacity from pastoralists and marginal farmers. We noted that these pressures were to some extent the effect of the commercialization of farming to the south of the Sahelian belt, and the changes in command over food resources as the relative incomes of pastoral and marginal farmers dropped. Within Latin America the high Andes is also resource-poor (although the inter-montane valleys are often fertile), and poverty can be attributed, quite plausibly, to the natural resource base. Again, we were able to distinguish structural factors which throw doubt on such an explanation. Land distribution in the Andean region is very unequal and large tracts of potentially arable land are laid to pasture by landlords. Increasingly, however, landlords have commercialized their holdings, expelled tenants and forced those with a land base onto marginal holdings. Agrarian reform, inasmuch as it has 'corrected' the skewed distribution of land, has accelerated rural proletarianization. Increasing proletarianization has contributed to poverty by placing more pressures on the land base and reducing the cost of 'free' wage labour to rural and urban employers. In the Latin American case differentiation mechanisms were internal and manifested through limited access to the environment, as well as heavier dependence on the market wage.

Countries such as India, Pakistan and Bangladesh possess a different agroclimatic and social structure. In most of monsoon Asia the land is worked intensively, irrigation is widely practised and a vast population is supported from the cultivation of rice paddy. In an influential study of Java, Clifford Geertz (1971) referred to the process whereby intensive rice cultivation adapted to increasing population growth on a limited land base, as 'agricultural involution'. Geertz made it clear that involution was the outcome of colonialism, but gave little attention to the formation of social classes in his analysis. Resource distribution was set against 'natural limits'. Important as it is, work like that of Geertz has fostered the widespread belief that in monsoon Asia poverty is simply the result of too many people or too little land.

Consider, for example, this section from the Brandt Commission Report, which deals with Bangladesh:

In Bangladesh, it has been estimated that one-third of the people are marginal peasants with less than one hectare of land, poor tenant farmers and share-croppers who are dependent on the larger land-holders for work. Another third of the population is estimated to be landless. *Land reform can only provide small relief for these people since large holdings account for only 0.2 per cent of the total land.* Investment in irrigation and flood control can provide the conditions for multiple crops which not only give increased yields but generate a much higher demand for labour.

(Brandt 1980: 86; my italics)

Without wishing to argue that land reform is a panacea for development problems in Bangladesh, this short passage begs some important questions. First, although it is true that large holdings are relatively unimportant in Bangladesh, the distribution of land has grown more unequal since the mid-1960s and landlessness has increased dramatically. As Clay suggests, 'if the objective is to eliminate poverty rather than alleviate it, there is no satisfactory alternative to assuring the landless a guaranteed share in the income stream from the one basic resource – land' (1981: 100). Such a prescription has advantages that neither increased rural public works nor grain purchases possess, and it would do more than relieve seasonal fluctuations in poverty.

In addition, the Brandt Commission may be more optimistic than is justified about the potential offered by improved irrigation and cropping techniques. As Clay maintains, the very large population that is supported at low levels of subsistence in Bangladesh is itself the outcome of 'cropping patterns . . . that reflect a very close adaptation to the existing environment' (1981: 93). Technological change has, in fact, served to maintain the poor, as well as producing substantial output growth since the early 1960s.

This last statement deserves careful explanation. Poverty in Bangladesh is closely linked with the growth of inequality in command over natural resources. Many of today's landless workers were formerly tenants of small farmers. An analysis of data on land sales prior to 1974, collected by the Bangladesh Institute of Development Studies, leads Sen to conclude:

one sees a clear bias towards land alienation on the part of the smaller landholders. The development not merely generally impoverished the group of small peasants; it also increased the ease with which members of the class could sink into starvation even in a year of relative plenty.

(1981: 151)

In a study for the ILO Rahman Khan argues that 'a very unfavourable average land endowment (only 0.3 acres of cultivable land per rural person . . .)' combined with 'a high degree of inequality' to produce 'an unprecedented concentration of extreme poverty in rural Bangladesh today' (Khan 1977: 137). Landlessness was precipitated by the adoption of new, high-yielding varieties of rice and the improved access of wealthier farmers to chemical inputs. Proletarianization of part of the rural population was matched by increasing differentiation of those who still retained land: 'the distribution of land among the remaining land-owners became less equal. An increasing proportion of landowners joined the category of small or "below subsistence" cultivators' (ibid.: 155).

There is, in addition, some evidence that landownership is more unequal than data from operational units would suggest, since the renting of land has replaced owner-occupation for many small farmers. In Bangladesh rural poverty is not a consequence of simple population pressure, but of the combined forces of accelerated technological change and a social structure rooted in inequality.

A recent examination of attitudes towards contraception in Bangladesh makes this point forcefully. Partly because of the official campaign of male sterilization and widely available contraceptives, family size among the poorest is gradually being reduced (IPPF 1982: 18). However, a Population Council working paper observes that the rural middle class still have large families: 'this is because wealth brings better health and money to keep the women in purdah, the traditional isolation of wives which encourages them to have more children' (ibid.: 18). Whereas technological change condemns most rural women to longer hours and excludes them from the benefits of development, it has enabled some rural women to bear more children and reinforce the status position of their husbands. Greater dependence on advanced agricultural technology has also increased the seasonal nutritional vulnerability of the poorest groups, especially women and children (Chowdury et al. 1981).

The implications of the rise in landlessness and the reduction in employment opportunities for many rural workers are not difficult to establish. The system of payment for rural workers has shifted with increasing proletarianization, from payments in kind to payments in cash. This increases the vulnerability of the poor and places a heavy burden on meeting food deficits through relief programmes. Data from the 1974 Bangladesh famine suggests that 81 per cent of those seeking food relief owned no land at all, or less than half an acre of land (Sen 1981: 144). There is reason to believe that future food shortages will hit the poor even harder as land concentrations, and the fall in real wages, proceed. Today, 46 per cent of Bangladesh's population of 90 million is under the age of fifteen. Within twenty-five years the population is expected to double to 180 million. The fertility of the land on the delta is matched by that of the population. A failure to recognize the role that better access to land can play in reducing human fertility will inevitably lead to continued destitution in rural areas, and increased dependence on international food aid.

Bangladesh illustrates precisely the need to consider resource endowments and population pressures together with structural changes induced by economic development. The gap between urban and rural living standards in Asia is frequently wider than that in Latin America, and has led some writers to attribute rural poverty to sectoral interests rather than those of class (Lipton 1977; Moore and Harriss 1984). Closer attention to the rural social structure reveals that the ownership and control of land has been instrumental in preserving the status of powerful landlords against the claims of other rural classes.

The watershed in Indian agrarian history came with the abolition of the *zamindars* and *jagirdars*, the absentee landlords who had acted as cultural intermediaries under British administration. With the removal of a feudal landowning class, the scene was set for the rich peasantry to establish itself on the rural stage. Prior to independence this class had been 'a class of capitalist farmers in embryo, in the womb of the old order' (Byres 1974: 235). The land that was distributed in *zamindar* areas after the demise of the *ancien régime* helped surviving landlords to accumulate more land, often by leasing it in, and thus increasing the size of their operational holdings. Attempts were made from the 1950s onwards to outlaw the more notorious forms of tenancy in Indian agriculture, but most rich and middle peasants adopted practices that enabled them to retain tenants but avoid the law.

At the time of independence in 1947 the category of 'poor peasants' was made up of operational holdings of up to 2 ha in size (Byres 1974: 233). By the 1970s it was calculated that between 3 and 5 ha was the minimum-sized holding able to provide a livelihood. However, in India and Pakistan the extent of rural landlessness was such that the amount of land available for each peasant was as little as 0.5 ha. In Bangladesh it was nearer 0.2 ha (Ward 1979: 181). Clearly the redistribution of land among the entire rural population, even if it was politically likely, would do little in itself to end rural poverty in the Indian sub-continent. The International Labour Office notes, in a study conducted in seven countries in Asia, that the degree of inequality was least in Bangladesh, but 'even there the bottom 20 per cent of the holdings account for only 3 per cent of the land while the top 10 per cent of the holdings account for over 35 per cent of the land' (ILO 1977: 11). Inequality in land distribution is growing in most parts of South-East Asia.

In India the view is usually taken that land reform should attempt to equalize the distribution of land among those who *already have access to it*. The landless enter into few land reform equations. Both rich peasants (kulaks) and poor peasants would oppose giving land to the landless. Caste is still an enduring part of Indian life and, as Bell observes, most of the landless are either Hindu outcastes or tribal peoples (Bell 1974: 197).

In the Indian sub-continent 'leasing-in' and 'leasing-out' arrangements are so common that landownership is not a sure guide to class position; something that it is, by and large, in most of Latin America. Operational holdings of the same size may vary greatly in the proportion of land owned, rather than leased-in (Beteille 1974). The 'ideal' Chayanovian situation where a peasant farmer neither depends on hire-labour from outside his family, nor hires out his own labour, is quite an exceptional one in most parts of India. Regional variation is also immense; women may be discouraged from working in the fields in some states, and agricultural labourers hired in their place. In other states women do agricultural work and there is thus less dependence on hired workers, even on quite large holdings (Beteille 1974).

One general pattern that can be discerned is the increase in landlessness. Byres notes that the conditions necessary for socioeconomic differentiation were created by the British: commodity production on an unprecedented scale, monetary values replacing non-monetary payment and land transferability (Byres 1974: 233). The stake which rich and middle peasants developed in the apportionment of land made further land reform increasingly unlikely: 'The present configuration of political forces in India effectively precludes redistribution: it is a configuration which derives from the agrarian structure which land reform, as implemented, has helped to create' (ibid.: 247). Between 1961 and 1971 the percentage of the total Indian workforce who were agricultural labourers rose from 16.7 to 25.8 (Bell 1974: 197). Beteille calculates that by 1971 some 40 per cent of those employed in agriculture were full-time labourers (Beteille 1974). In states like Andhra Pradesh and Kerala agricultural labourers were more numerous than peasant cultivators.

These dramatic changes in the agrarian structure, attributable to changes in the size and quality of holdings, as well as the tenurial status of their cultivation, were partly the effect of the introduction of new agricultural technologies, the 'Green Revolution'. Under rapid technological change access to technical inputs assumes much more importance. Not surprisingly rich peasants, and to a lesser extent, middle peasants, have adopted such innovations much more readily and intensively than poor peasants and tenants (Bell 1974: 205). Since the early 1970s the scale of rural differentiation has continued unabated (Pearse 1980). Even writers who have drawn attention to the pro-equity advantages of the 'Green Revolution', such as Lipton, agree that 'non-technical relationships affecting High Yielding Varieties and associated input use . . . generally [favour] bigger farmers' (Lipton 1978: 321).

One of the crucial questions raised by land ceiling legislation in India, and made more urgent as the 'Green Revolution' spread, is whether or not a reduction in equality among farm operators increases the inequality between them and the landless. Bell argues that the evidence is by no means clear (1974: 208). Lipton notes that 'in one way High Yielding Varieties and land reform involve a similar dilemma: acts that redistribute from big to small farmers may tend to redistribute against farm labourers'. He concludes that the outcome depends on policy towards mechanization and irrigation, which determines which way the balance of advantage falls (1978: 330).

The development possibilities presented by areas of smallholding agriculture can be appreciated by reference to Japan, Taiwan and Korea, all of which have experienced distributive land reforms. In each of these countries twice as many workers are employed per hectare as in India or Pakistan (Ward 1979: 181). The productivity of these smallholdings owes a great deal to appropriate mechanization and the relative ease with which rural credit and chemical inputs are obtained. Even without adequate credit and mechanization double or treble cropping and flood control are potentially important ways of increasing agricultural productivity on the smallest holding. In China the individual or household plots occupy between 5 and 8 per cent of the co-operatively farmed agricultural land, but account for between 9 and 30 per cent of family income (Bergmann 1977: 142).

POOR ENVIRONMENTS OR ENVIRONMENTAL POVERTY?

Poverty often occurs in resource-poor environments. The dry Sahel and the high Andes are examples of such environments. But is the delta of Bangladesh a poor environment? Clearly poverty in Bangladesh, as in many parts of monsoon Asia, is the outcome of a relatively rich resource base helping to maintain a large human population. By contrast, poverty in the Andes can be attributed to the marginalization of the poor, their alienation from land. Even in the case of the Sahel it is difficult to attribute poverty to poor resources alone. Changes in the *relative* position of pastoralists and poor farmers, within a supranational context, account for the poverty of the Sahelian population.

Can we, therefore, safely assume that poverty is the result of economic forces and distributive processes? In each of the cases we considered, distributive mechanisms – land concentration, the decline in real wages, capital accumulation – contributed to rural poverty. Clearly, resource-poor areas are resource-poor partly because of structural processes.

However, the inhabitants of poor environments are not poor simply because they are allocated too little land. Their 'misuse' of their environments is enforced and traceable to their poverty. They both receive a smaller 'share' of natural resources and make excessive demands of the 'share' they receive. These might be described as the 'proximate' and 'underlying' causes of rural poverty, and need to be distinguished analytically, just as they are compounded in real life.

Poverty is everywhere the outcome of specific relations between the natural environment and socioeconomic structures. To ignore the specificity of these relations, to equate poverty in the Sahel with poverty in the Andes or Bangladesh, is to reason from outcome to causes, *a posteriori*. Human poverty makes physical environments poorer, just as poor physical environments make for greater human poverty. What needs to be recognized is the specificity of the relationship between structural factors and those of the natural environment. In the next chapter we focus on one country, Mexico, and consider how the conflicts emerging within the Mexican countryside have led to the introduction of new policies. We shall see that the structural factors which compound environmental poverty also make it difficult to frame policies to ensure sustainable development.

5

Environmental conflict and development policy in rural Mexico

Most of the discussion in previous chapters has been conducted at the level of comparison. A conscious attempt has been made to suggest links between the role of ideology in development and the recourse that is made to the natural environment. Casting the net very widely, the problems confronting the environment in the South have been considered in ways that lend themselves to comparative interpretation and analysis. Illustrative material has been drawn from Asia, Africa and Latin America giving consideration to the specificities of each continent's historical experience. To some extent such an approach is made inevitable by the nature of the subject; the environmental crisis is both international and interdisciplinary. Ways out of the crisis require new approaches to the conventional boundaries forged by academic disciplines.

This chapter departs from this emphasis on generalizable theory by focusing on one country, Mexico, and considering environmental and food policies within the context provided by Mexico's development experience. It begins by analysing a new development strategy which was adopted by the Mexican government in May 1980. This strategy was called the 'Mexican Food System' (*Sistema Alimentario Mexicano*, or SAM) and was intended to reverse the direction of Mexico's rural development towards greater self-sufficiency in basic foods and the better conservation of rural resources. The discussion which ensued raised many of the issues which radical ecology and political economy have raised about rural development in general. Specifically, it concerned the role of different interpretations of development in helping to frame environmental and food policy.

The problems of Mexican rural development are understood differently by different groups of people. One group, which we can loosely term *campesinistas* (pro-peasant) believes that poverty in rural Mexico is a result of the way the peasant farmer has been treated by government and rural bosses (*caciques*) and that more attention needs to be paid to the way in which traditional farming systems utilize scarce natural resources. From the Left of Mexican politics emerges a slightly different analysis: the underdevelopment and poverty of rural regions is attributable to international economic relations. In this view, Mexico's economic dependency on the United States has impoverished rural people in the interest of multinational corporations and agribusiness. The rural class structure is a reflection of these international development processes. The analysis presented in the 'SAM', although not the policies, rested on a combination of these two views.

However, a third view of Mexican development can also be identified, although it is rarely advocated publicly, since it conflicts with much of the 'revolutionary' rhetoric that is still current in Mexico. This view is that there are too many people on the land, not too few. Bureaucracy and paternalistic politics have disguised the inefficiency of Mexican agriculture, while the corruption of peasant leaders and government personnel has reduced agricultural productivity. By contrast, the most modern sectors of agriculture, particularly in the irrigated zones of the country, are efficiently managed and make better use of the 'comparative advantages' conferred on Mexico by her climate and proximity to the United States. This 'developmentalist' perspective echoes the concerns of neo-classical economics.

INTERPRETATIONS OF MEXICAN RURAL DEVELOPMENT

At the beginning of this chapter a number of rival interpretations of Mexican rural development are set out. Subsequently these interpretations are elaborated upon and we examine the problems that each approach raises.

The *campesinistas*, we have noted, were dedicated to the idea that Mexican development had been prejudicial to the interests of the large mass of rural people, the peasant farmers. Commercial agriculture – especially irrigated agriculture – had benefited from government subsidies and generous public investment. By contrast, government agencies in the poorer, 'rain-fed' regions of Mexico, had succeeded in exploiting the peasant farmer, making him pay for agricultural development by offering low prices for his crops and profiting from the cheap labour of his family. The peasant family was thus exploited *structurally* under Mexican development policy.

The proponents of an alternative 'peasant led' policy also draw attention to the importance of the peasant's experience in agriculture, most of which is systematically ignored. Some commentators suggest that peasant 'farming systems' should form the basis for an alternative agronomy, less dependent on bought inputs, such as fertilizers and insecticides and more attuned to the existing natural resources and climatic conditions of rural Mexico (Turrent 1979). The peasant's 'experience' has also been emphasized by anthropologists like Warman, who argues that the very fact that the peasant economy cannot be completely destroyed testifies to its importance (Warman 1976).

The political struggle being waged by the Mexican peasantry, according to the *campesinistas*, is on two fronts. First, it is still a struggle for land, since the promise of the Revolution to return the land to those who worked it has not been met. Indeed, there is evidence that land distribution in rural Mexico is as unequal now as it was in 1910 (Hewitt 1976). Second, the attempts made by peasant farmers to improve their livelihoods are blocked at every turn by middlemen and urban merchants, who lend at high interest rates and seek to monopolize the handling of basic grains in many remote areas of rural Mexico. The *campesinistas* themselves are divided as to whether the Mexican state can effectively dislodge these middlemen or *caciques*, while offering the peasantry some of the services they provide at a less exploitative level (Redclift 1980).

There are a number of weaknesses in the argument presented by the pro-peasant lobby. It is not altogether clear how the Mexican state can forge a better relationship with the *campesinos* when the history of its dealings with them has been so ambivalent. To this objection some Marxists would add two others. If the continued co-existence of the peasant economy and capitalism has so impoverished the peasantry, what is there to suggest that it *could* be different? *Campesinista* writers like Esteva have always insisted that the welfare of the peasantry is not inconsistent with the continued existence of industrial capitalism. The Marxist camp also challenges a central tenet of the *campesinistas* in arguing that wage-labour has developed within Mexican agriculture to the point where it is impossible to speak about a 'peasantry' at all. Peasant-led rural development without a peasantry is an absurdity.

The factual evidence adduced by the Marxists coincides with that of the *campesinistas* in a number of respects. The interpretation diverges in several ways, however. First, as we have seen, the claim is made that rural proletarianization has developed to the point where a peasantry no longer exists in Mexico. The links with the land, especially the *ejido* which *campesinistas* see as evidence of 'peasantness', are interpreted differently by Marxists. They see the 'peasant' household's dependence on wages earned off the landholding as much more important to its class position (Paré 1977).

The Marxist view of agrarian reform also diverges from that of the *campesinistas*. Sociologists like Gutelman and Roger Bartra have argued that the maintenance of peasant farming was essential to the successful evolution of capitalism in Mexico after the Revolution (Gutelman 1974; Bartra 1974). The *ejido* preserved the idea of private property in land, and rather than keep faith with the agrarian aspirations of Zapata's followers, succeeding Mexican Presidents (including Cárdenas) were responsible for restructuring Mexican rural society in the interests of capital. The boost given commercial farming by the state was the logical outcome of taking a capitalist road to rural development. The peasantry was not so much ignored as tailored to this model. Today, Mexican agriculture evolves according to the logic of the 'international division of labour' – producing cheap fruit and vegetables for the United States market, and cheap labour, much of it employed illegally, to the north of the Rio Grande.

The Marxist position has weaknesses, too. The alternative to private landownership is collective agriculture which, as we have seen, usually does not receive widespread support in rural Mexico. Assuming that the agricultural sector does yield a 'surplus' to industry, by depressing the peasant's standard of living, it remains unclear how collectivization would both improve living standards in rural areas *and* yield the necessary surplus for industry. Meeting peasant land claims might make political sense, but would it provide the help needed for Mexico's poorest rural groups and the stimulus which the economy needs?

The third major critique of Mexican rural development is that of the 'developmentalist' school of orthodox neoclassical economists. This is the view favoured by most foreign interests in Mexico, including the private banks, multinational food companies and firms interested in exploiting Mexico's petroleum resources. The view of this 'Radical Right' is rarely aired in the Mexican media, but as events showed during and after the currency crisis in the summer of 1982, orthodox neoclassical thinking is still very important. The most coherent expression of this view is that of Lamartine Yates, who argues that the political guarantees extended to the peasantry after the Revolution have actually hindered Mexico's rural development (Yates 1981). The role of the Mexican state has been to distort the working of market forces. Land was thus dedicated to unsuitable crops, and absorbed too much of the rural population, where labour was surplus to the requirements of capital. Technological efficiency has been sacrificed for political stability. Mexico, according to this view, should concentrate on those products for which it has a 'comparative advantage'. These are precisely those products (oil seeds, fruit and cash crops like cotton) which Marxists and *campesinistas* alike think of as having contributed, by their cultivation, to structural inequality in rural areas. The principal query about the 'developmental-ist' position is thus: if rural poverty cannot be reduced by adopting 'market' criteria for agricultural policy, what guarantee is there that increased emphasis on economic growth through relying on market forces will not further increase structural inequalities?

When the SAM proposals were first introduced most people concerned with rural development planning applauded them. The support given to the proposals by most people on the Left needs explanation, however. The view seemed to be that rocking the boat might lead to a reaction in favour of the Right, while a 'wait-and-see' approach might enable a head of steam to be built up in support of the new proposals. The magnitude of the food crisis facing Mexico persuaded most people interested in public policy that a departure from previous policy was worth a try. It soon became clear that the SAM would not resolve the structural problems of Mexico's rural sector, although short-term gains were likely. In 1981 the harvest was good and the production goals of the SAM were met. The following year, 1982, the harvest was worse and the political initiative moved towards those who supported the new President-elect, de la Madrid. The economic crisis of the summer and autumn 1982 was met by fairly orthodox financial measures designed to reassure the International Monetary Fund of Mexico's ability to put its house in order. The SAM, once a brave initiative, was soon quietly forgotten.

THE SAM: NEW DIRECTIONS IN FOOD AND ENVIRONMENT POLICY

SAM provides Mexico with an opportunity perhaps unique and unrepeatable, to satisfy our great potential for growth of the food system without making unnecessary concessions to sovereignty, without being strangled by external attachments of financial servitude.

(Jose Lopez Portillo, President of Mexico, 18 March 1980)

Using these words the Mexican President announced a new policy to return Mexico to self-sufficiency in basic foods, and address the stark problems of rural poverty in many areas of the country. Why was such a policy necessary, seventy years after the first Revolution of the twentieth century had given land to the tiller? In answering this question we need to begin by undertaking a survey of rural Mexico at the beginning of the 1980s (see *Table 3*).

Table 3 Mexico's rural sector

---

1 *Cultivated land (1978)*
    (a) rain-fed area   11,262,000 ha
    (b) irrigated area   3,176,000 ha

                       Total   14,438,000 ha

Source: Dept of Programing and Budget, Mexican government 1978.

---

2 *Principal crops (1980)*   *% distribution*
   food staples (corn, wheat, beans)   59% of cultivated area
                             (20% of total value)
   forage crops (sorghum, alfalfa, etc.)   11% of cultivated area
                             (16% of total value)
   fruit and vegetables   7% of cultivated area
                             (20% of total value)
   others (coffee, tobacco, oil seeds, etc.)   23% of cultivated area
                             (44% of total value)

Source: Dept of Programing and Budget, Mexican government 1980.

---

3 *Crop Land: annual rates of growth in food crops and forage crops (1965–79)*

Basic food crops %		Forage crops %	
maize	−1.75	alfalfa	5.5
beans	−6.15	oats	26.5
wheat	−2.3	barley	18.8
		sorghum	15.0

Source: D. Barkin 1981: 22.

---

4 *Land tenure (1970)*

	% of land area
ejidos	43
independent communities	7
private farms	50

Source: Ministry of Agriculture, Mexican government 1971.

	No. of families (1970)
peasant farmers (*ejidos*)	1,600,000
peasant farmers (independent communities)	200,000
private farmers	600,000
hired workers, seasonal and full-time	900,000
	3,300,000

Source: Yates 1981: 146.

---

5 *Mexico: Maize and wheat imports (1960–1980) as % of total consumption*

	Maize	Wheat
1960	0.5	—
1970	8.6	—
1980	34.2	18.1

Source: Mexican government 1981.

Most of Mexico's cultivated land is not irrigated. The 3 million ha or so of land that are irrigated are located primarily in the north-west and north of the country, where extensive public works were undertaken in the 1950s and 1960s. Few of the rural people live in these areas, however. Most live in the 'rain-fed' regions, where agriculture is in the hands of peasant producers and their families. Such people worked over 11 million ha of land in 1978 (see *Table 3*).

Most of the rain-fed areas of Mexico are prone to drought or unreliable rainfall. As Figure 1 shows, the bulk of the rural population inhabits the central plateau and mountain area, where rainfall is relatively poor. The humid tropics to the south enjoy reliable rainfall, but fewer people live there.

For most peasant producers the staple crops are maize and beans, and *Table 3* shows us that these crops and wheat (which is grown principally in the irrigated areas) take up almost 60 per cent of the cultivated land area. During the last twenty years, and particularly during the last decade, other crops have assumed importance. In 1980 forage crops, for feeding to animals, covered 11 per cent of the cultivated land area and accounted for 16 per cent of crop values. Other crops, including fruit and vegetables, coffee and tobacco account for 30 per cent of the cultivated land area and almost two-thirds of the market value of all the crops grown. The growth in forage crop production, in particular, is clear from the figures for the period 1965–79 in the table.

During the 1970s Mexican agriculture showed a decline in basic food-crops, largely at the expense of crops for animal feeds and for export to the United States. Animal products are only consumed by a minority of relatively affluent people in Mexico, and much of the fruit and vegetables grown are sent directly to California, Texas and other places during the winter period when their own production falls off. Cash crops like coffee and tobacco are important income-earners for Mexico, but the benefit they provide the balance of payments is not passed on to the rural poor. As *Table 3* shows, in 1980 Mexico had reduced its self-sufficiency in basic foodcrops to a point where a third of its requirements were being met by imports. Even wheat was being imported on a large scale, despite the 'miracle' Green Revolution seeds being used in the irrigated north-west. At the same time Mexico was feeding its middle-class rather better, exporting fruit and 'winter vegetables' very successfully and raising more cattle for the hamburger 'chains' in North America.

The condition of most rural people in Mexico provides a vivid contrast with the 'successes' of commercial agriculture. *Table 3* indicates that over 40 per cent of the cultivated land area in Mexico was worked as *ejidos*, or communally owned land. The *ejido* was introduced after the

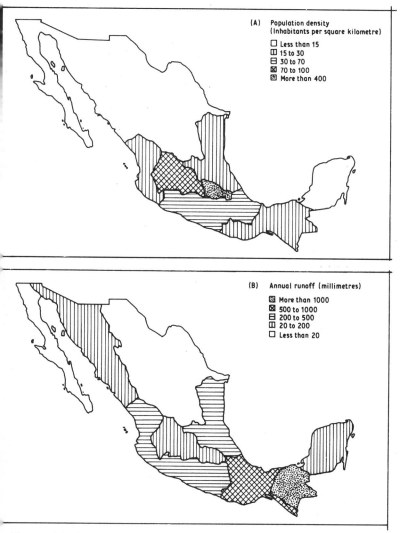

Figure 1 A basic problem confronting agricultural planners in Mexico is that the distribution of the population (*map A*) does not coincide with the distribution of the water resources (*map B*). Thus most of the people (and most of the farms) are concentrated in the drier areas of the country, particularly in the central highlands, which have more than half of the population but only about 10 per cent of the water resources. In contrast, approximately 40 per cent of the country's available water supply is in the humid south-eastern region, where only about 8 per cent of the people live. The two maps on this page are based on data obtained by the Mexican Ministry of Hydraulic Resources; for comparative statistical purposes the country is divided on both of the maps into 13 major hydrologic regions.

Source: E. Wellhausen, 'The agriculture of Mexico', *Scientific American*, vol. 235 (1976), no. 3.

Revolution to provide a land base for the peasantry, which had largely been dispossessed of land by large farmers and speculators, many of them foreign. *Ejidos* are rarely collectively worked, and most of the land is divided into small plots worked by individual families. During the 1930s a collectivization programme was begun under President Cárdenas but these policies were reversed by Cárdenas' successors. Today, most peasant farmers on *ejido* land need to earn income from other sources to sustain their families. Consequently, they migrate regularly across the border to the United States, or to other parts of Mexico for seasonal employment in agriculture. Many *ejido* peasants maintain close links with urban centres, where they or their children find casual work for part of the year.

The heading 'private farmers' in *Table 3* covers a multiple of farming classes. Some work small- or medium-size farms; Mexicans call them *rancheros* and they played a significant part in Mexican history (Schryer 1980; Brading 1978). The most important group, however, are the large commercial farmers, some of them also government officials or beneficiaries of the Revolution in its earlier phases. The interests of this group are inextricably linked with export production and the United States. In some crops, such as strawberries and citrus fruits, North American companies are heavily involved in Mexican agriculture.

The number of hired workers is probably much greater than suggested by the figures in *Table 3*. As we saw, many *ejido* peasants work away from their land plots. The agricultural census figures also under-represent women and children, who play a large part in seasonal employment picking coffee and tobacco, cotton and fruit. Women and children are the poorest and most exploited section of Mexico's rural population.

It is clear from these figures, inadequate as they are, that at least half of Mexico's rural population is dependent on wages, often earned at some distance from home. The Revolution that promised land to those who worked it had succeeded by 1980 in removing a significant section from the land altogether. Those who did work the land were very unlikely to receive outside technical assistance, credit for buying fertilizers and seeds or help with marketing their produce. These critical functions were in the hands of intermediaries and rural bosses called *caciques* or *coyotes* by Mexicans.

Three-fifths of the *ejidos* in Mexico received no official government credit in 1980. They constituted about 71 per cent of the cultivated land. Despite this fact the Mexican government's credit bank, Banrural, distributed over one billion United States dollars' worth of agricultural credit in 1979, an increase of 32 per cent over 1978. Since most of Banrural's credit goes to small producers (the private banks look after the bigger farmers) the bulk of official credit must go to a minority of relatively rich peasant farmers, some of them on irrigated land. Improving the situation of poor *ejido* farmers was one of the goals of the SAM.

The SAM was introduced because of an awareness of the deepening crisis over food production, and the increasing evidence that other forms of state intervention in rural Mexico had not helped the poorest rural groups. However, not everybody within the presidential administration of Lopez Portillo was convinced of the need for a new direction in policy. Indeed, within a year of the policy's introduction a new Agricultural Development Law was passed (*Ley de Fomento Agropecuario*) which appeared to favour large farmers rather than the poor peasantry and enabled critics of the SAM to argue that the government was proceeding in two different directions at the same time (Redclift 1981a).

It remains to outline the policy measures proposed under the SAM, and the way in which they were intended to work. Basically, the SAM was a package of related policies drawn up after initial research by over twenty committees. The proposals were intended to achieve three objectives: to increase domestic production of strategically important food crops (maize, beans, rice and sugar); to streamline food delivery systems serving the urban and rural poor; and to improve the nutrition of vulnerable target groups in both areas. Specific measures included raising the price of corn by 31 per cent and beans by 25 per cent, so that peasant farmers would be encouraged to grow and sell these crops rather than turn to other crops, or abandon the land altogether. Improved seeds would be made available to poor farmers and they were promised the free delivery of 600,000 tons of fertilizer at prices 20 per cent below commercial rates (Meissner 1981). Resources for combating plant diseases were to be increased and the cost of crop insurance reduced for the peasant farmer. Perhaps most important of all, agricultural credit policy was redesigned with the interests of the maize-producing farmer in mind, freeing him from exploitative intermediaries.

Efforts were also made to improve food delivery systems. Sections of the food industry that collaborated with the SAM were given a financial boost by the injection of state funds. Specifically, the SAM strove 'to encourage vertically integrated agricultural undertakings which would combine labour intensive agricultural production with capital intensive transformation processes' (Meissner 1981: 223). More agribusiness was placed under government control.

The nutritional elements in the policy package were in some ways the most innovative. It was calculated that about 35 million Mexicans, more than half the country's population, failed to reach *per capita* daily food

intakes of 2750 calories and 80 g of protein. Of this number over half –
13 million in rural areas and 6 million in cities – were estimated to have
fallen well below these 'minimum' nutritional levels. The most vulnerable were rural women and children, whose nutritional levels would be
improved through subsidizing a Recommended Basic Food Basket,
reducing its cost to poor consumers to about 13 Mexican *pesos* per day
per head. (This was about 26p in January 1980.)

The SAM recognized that to reach the target population it was necessary
to increase the number and efficiency of the retail outlets used by poor
people, especially those of the government's food distribution organization, CONASUPO. In the cities poor people tended to use small grocery
stores or public markets, many of which were mobile (*mercados sobre
ruedas*: 'markets on wheels'). Different prices were established for specific
marketing channels, enabling the state's subsidy to be relatively selective.

Such an ambitious development programme was only possible because
Mexico was in the fortunate, and rather unusual, position of having
enormous petroleum reserves. By 1980 it was the world's fifth largest oil
producer, and the country's potential reserves were ranked second only
to Saudi Arabia's. In 1938 under President Cárdenas the Mexican
government had nationalized the petroleum industry and PEMEX, the
government's oil monopoly, was linked with the nationalist aspirations
of both Left and Right. In 1980 the subsidies received by the SAM
amounted to almost $4 billion. This could easily be financed from oil
income. After all, if one million barrels of oil were sold each day (which
was well within capacity), at a price of US $40 a barrel, it would yield
approximately $14.6 billion a year. The Mexicans, following on the
heels of the Venezuelans in the early 1970s, were 'sowing their petroleum' by ploughing back oil revenues into rural development (Meissner 1981). On the face of it such a strategy had everything to recommend
it. In the following section we will consider the principal obstacle to its
success; the role that the Mexican state had come to play in the rural
sector. The paradox is unavoidable. Mexico alone in Latin America had
the means to develop its rural sector rapidly and effectively. But it had
also inherited a burden of suspicion and corruption which hampered any
initiative taken at the top of the political system.

THE MEXICAN STATE AND RURAL DEVELOPMENT

At the beginning of this chapter it was suggested that the Mexican state
bureaucracy might not be equipped to deal with the problems of rural
development, either technically or politically. It is important to look at
the extent to which rural development policy can be implemented.

The ability and experience of Mexico's public sector is probably greater than in most other Latin American countries. Mexico possesses many highly-trained civil servants and planners, and the scope provided by the country's development has enabled many of these people to gain valuable experience of policymaking and policy implementation. Food policy, in particular, had been recognized as of critical importance by public functionaries before the SAM was introduced (Grindle 1977; Esteva 1980).

Implementing public policy is not a purely 'technical' question, however. The degree to which a government is committed to a policy will vary widely in specific cases. In Mexico, presidents frequently support two or more teams of researchers and civil servants within the same policy area. Each team reports directly to the president and he decides which will be given the green light. Frequently the president's support for one team is conditional on its achieving certain goals, and he is liable to 'change horses' midway through the six-year presidential term or *sexenio*.

Within government agencies personal support from the president is of critical importance and the careers of most civil servants follow that of a political patron to whom they became attached early on. The future of the civil servant or professional in the public sector is dictated by the fortunes of 'leaders', every bit as much as the peasant or urban shantytown dweller. Lomnitz sums up these leadership roles in the following way:

> The leader is a broker who derives resources from his articulation with the larger structure, and who distributes a share of these resources to each follower according to rank. In return, each client contributes services and loyalty to his superior, according to his closeness to the leader. The flow of loyalty towards the leader determines the social cohesion or solidarity within the group. (1982: 65)

One of the difficulties in assessing the 'technical' ability of the Mexican state to confront development problems is that much of the effort of people working in government goes into maintaining their personal position within the bureaucracy, rather than implementing agreed policy.

In addition, the gestation period for government policy in Mexico is determined not by any 'objective' considerations derived from the policy itself, but by the sequence of events which make up a *sexenio* or presidential term. Merilee Grindle describes this timeframe very vividly in her book about CONASUPO, the government agency concerned with the marketing and processing of basic foods:

> The influence of the *sexenio* on CONASUPO was clear, and the patterns of behaviour it encouraged are repeated in hundreds of other

public agencies in Mexico with predictable regularity. At the beginning of each presidential term, bureaucratic agencies are assigned
leaders who must then set about learning the intricacies of their new
responsibilities. Soon they begin to replace the middle and top level
officials who have remained, uncertain and virtually inactive, from the
previous administration. At the same time, the new managers evaluate
the organizations they have acquired and attempt to introduce revised
policies and new programmes. This process takes time. A year or more
might go by before a satisfactory team has been recruited; another six
or twelve months might be devoted to study, reorganization, and
policy development. During this period, the regular functions of the
organizations are reduced to a minimal level as 'old' administrators
equivocate and 'new' ones acquire experience.   (1977: 165)

From this account we can gain some idea of the difficulty of changing the
course of development policy in the light of experience at implementing
it. Not surprisingly most professionals and administrators are at pains to
demonstrate the success of a policy. This is true anywhere in the world.
However, in Mexico, the opportunity to carry out policy is confined,
effectively, to about one-third of each six-year presidential term. Within
this restricted timeframe public policy can only work if the president's
ear is 'bent' by somebody close to him at the critical moment.

We are moving almost imperceptibly from a discussion of the 'technical' element in development policy to an account of its political viability.
As we have seen, the *qualitative* aspects of social relations within the
Mexican bureaucracy make it difficult to establish whether there is a
basis to state-assisted rural development. Nowhere is this more important than in the practice of corruption, which plays an important role in
the implementation of rural development in Mexico.

During the 1970s the most important programme for rural development in Mexico was PIDER (Programme for Integrated Rural Development). This programme started in 1973, when it covered forty-three so-
called 'micro-regions' with a total population of 2.4 million people. By
1978 PIDER 'micro-regions' covered almost one-fifth of Mexico's rural
population: 5 million people. Within these 'micro-regions' PIDER
attempted to integrate the functions of different government agencies. It
was a pioneering effort, which was supported with some enthusiasm by
the World Bank (IBRD 1979). The programme embraced almost any
kind of project from rabbit production at the individual family level, to
dairy farming units comprising over three hundred milk cows. Also
within PIDER were irrigation projects of different sizes, nutrition and
preventative health courses and support for commercial fruit growing.

Apart from 'integrating' what government agencies did in specific targeted areas, PIDER sought to gain the support of the local population for its projects (IBRD 1983). An office was established to evaluate the progress of PIDER projects and make recommendations for fuller public participation. However, not until the programme was well established did it become clear that local people often did not want the kind of projects favoured by the government officials (IBRD 1983). Local participation was an afterthought, rather than the driving force of the programme.

The failure of many rural development efforts is reflected in the indifference with which rural people have responded to outside 'development'. Often nobody had asked the local people what they wanted. Second, the budget for construction companies undertaking public works regularly includes bribes to public officials to ensure that the work is done. They are thus able to report to their seniors that the project has been completed, regardless of whether or not it is useful, or even being used. Villages exist throughout Mexico where drinking water systems have been built, in line with published policy, but in which the water has never been connected. The bribes or *mordidas* ('little bites') that oil the wheels of bureaucracy do not necessarily distribute resources fairly, and are often wasteful. They also reduce the credibility of government officials, whose disinterest cannot be assumed. Not surprisingly, poor rural people often treat government officials with indifference or, by emulating their behaviour, make the problems of implementing rural development even more intractable. Projects in rural Mexico are often conceived to generate money for political clients or pay off political patrons. They are rarely responsive to local needs or managed by local people.

The other 'side' of the coin represented by paternalism and government corruption is that of the peasantry itself. The livelihoods of many poor rural people are very precarious. Their production strategy is designed to reduce risks, rather than increase profits. This 'mentality' is logical, but its logic often eludes professional experts from the cities. Thus, suspicion of government officials is often combined with mutual incomprehension, as the criteria for helping the rural poor through agricultural credit, for example, are essentially banking criteria far removed from the workings of the household production unit. Where the peasant farmer is becoming 'proletarianized', becoming progressively more dependent on wages than on his land, he may seek a solution to his poverty in demands for more access to land. However, those poor farmers with land are more likely to resist all interference from the state. This is the face of peasant 'conservatism' so often decried by middle-class professionals.

If the state does little to ensure better co-operation among poor farmers, it is hardly surprising that the farmers themselves should be so suspicious of government attempts to encourage co-operative or collectivist agriculture. The story is the same throughout rural Mexico, from the dry irrigated regions of the north-west (Hewitt 1976; Winder 1977) to the tropical basins, where studies such as that of Plan Chontalpa (Barkin 1978; Bartra 1976) and the Papaloapan Basin (Ewell and Poleman 1980) document the collusion of a minority of peasants with government, to the exclusion of the poorest and most vulnerable. In each case the Mexican state has urged 'co-operation' upon a seemingly apathetic peasantry, which is determined if at all possible, to work land on a family-household basis free from government controls. Non-government organizations which have worked closely with peasant farmers in Mexico, such as the Mexican Foundation for Rural Development, draw attention to the peasant farmer's lack of 'accountability'. He is not used to being accountable for what he does with public money. The principles behind the allocation of government funds have more to do with whom he knows than with his efficiency or productivity.

It is clear from what has been written that we cannot separate the 'technical' from the 'political' aspects of rural development in Mexico. It is also clear that the political system within which policy is formulated and implemented works through by-passing formal structures in allocating resources. Clearly, the relationship between the Mexican state and peasantry has militated *against* creating a social base capable of supporting and implementing the SAM. The existing social and political alignments in the Mexican countryside are incompatible with the role which the SAM expects of state agencies. We might also ask whether they are incompatible with new rural resource uses in the Mexican countryside.

CHANGES IN THE RURAL ENVIRONMENT

So far, we have analysed rural development by examining the structural roots of Mexico's food crisis. We noted that although Mexico's petroleum reserves enabled an alternative food and environmental policy to be financed, there were a number of question marks over the state's ability to implement the new policy. In this section we turn from an examination of the social and political basis of Mexican rural development to consider the natural resource endowments in different ecological regions, and the effect of social and economic pressures on this resource base. This analysis raises two specific questions. Could existing resources be exploited more productively *without* a major change in Mexico's economic and social structure? Can the social classes who own and control these natural resources be expected to favour new resource uses?

Highland rain-fed areas

A basic distinction is made in Mexican rural development circles between 'rain-fed' and irrigated agriculture. However, the category 'rain-fed' agriculture is a wide one. Only about 30 to 40 per cent of Mexico's rain-fed agriculture receives enough rainfall (750 mm per annum and less than 35 per cent probability of drought) for improved maize varieties to be grown successfully. If soils are good and rainfall relatively reliable, land can have enormous production potential. This was the case in the area covered by Plan Puebla (1967–73), an agricultural extension project designed to help peasant farmers acquire credit with which to buy fertilizers and improved seed varieties (CIMMYT 1974). According to one authority, if other relatively well-endowed areas received similar assistance, Mexican maize production could be trebled (Wellhausen 1976).

The peasant farmers who work land in favoured rain-fed regions are not rich. But many of them can expect to receive increased attention from Mexican government agronomists and lending agencies. One private organization, the Mexican Foundation for Rural Development, increased its agricultural credit five-fold during the period 1975–9. Most of this credit went to the top strata of peasant farmers. This process is sometimes referred to as 'commoditization', since the farmer is producing largely for the market rather than personal consumption. Urban growth ensures that the demand for basic foods such as maize, beans and chillies, will continue in Mexico, and the 'commoditized' peasant farmer is likely to attract more and more assistance from government and private sectors. In a sense, the SAM merely hastened this process.

By contrast, most of Mexico's rural poor also live in the highland rain-fed regions of the country. Banrural, the government's agricultural credit bank, assesses the number of 'seriously under-employed' at about five million people. The Ministry of Agriculture and Water Resources estimates that about 40 per cent of Mexico's rural population is in this category. Most of these people are still producers of basic crops, but increasingly they consume more than they can produce themselves. The shortfall has to be made up by working for wages, or in the so-called 'informal sector' of cities, wherever casual employment is found. These people can be expected to continue to desert the land for most of the year, while retaining a nominal interest in the continuation of the *ejido* land unit.

The implications of the demographic and social structure of rural regions for land use are not difficult to perceive. Many rural Mexicans continue to want better access to land in the areas where the resource base cannot support the existing population. Casual work in commercial agriculture, the cities or across the border, does not represent an alternative to the *ejido* but complements it. The resource-poor areas of rural Mexico cannot be 'rationalized' so as to provide better livelihoods for those who spend most of their lives there, without re-awakening land hunger in those who exist, precariously, by keeping a toe-hold in the *ejido*. The attempts at creating alternative employment, such as the *maquiladoras* or component-shops established along the Mexican-United States border, have had little effect in increasing male employment opportunities. Like the strawberry packing plants in Michoacan, or the fruit-canneries in Montemorelos, they attract young female workers, underpaid and living with their families (Arizpe and Arandes 1981). The prognosis for the highland 'peasant' region of Mexico is bleak. Some people might prosper in resource-rich zones, but the mass of the population cannot make more effective use of the poor land and water resources available to them.

Irrigated regions

The irrigated regions of Mexico produce most of the country's wheat, as well as cash crops such as cotton, tobacco, fruit and vegetables. One of the principal objectives of the SAM was to reverse the balance of advantages currently enjoyed by the irrigation zones. Between 1950 and 1970, more than 70 per cent of the federal government's expenditure on agriculture was devoted to irrigation projects (Esteva 1975: 1313). In 1979 the maintenance and extension of existing irrigation infrastructure still accounted for 41 per cent of the total agricultural budget (*Review of Economic Situation of Mexico* 1979: 251). Clearly, the Mexican state is heavily committed to supporting the irrigated zones financially, whatever new directions are being launched in food policy.

Irrigation systems suffer from major technical problems, notably salinization, and their upkeep is expensive. To ensure reliable water supplies irrigation officials need to be bribed, and politicians tend to be responsive to the needs of the larger users (Wade 1979). Most of the benefits accrue to those who can obtain inputs cheaply, and sell their product through established marketing channels. In Mexico these rich farmers – some of whom work *ejido* land – have prospered. Cynthia Hewitt, in her study of Sonora, showed how patterns of consumption were important in concentrating wealth into fewer hands. Some farmers had become indebted as a result of the failure of their own farming efforts. These debts were compounded by others, contracted in order to buy consumption goods and services (Hewitt 1976). The new levels of agricultural investment and output in Mexico's north-west have increased inequality, although the abject poverty of some other regions is rarely observed (Mujica 1978).

Most of the products of the irrigated regions are destined for export or consumption by the relatively large Mexican middle class. The competitive position of irrigated agriculture thus depends on combining low wage costs with favourable growing conditions. Since the demand for high value foodstuffs is unlikely to fall, and the SAM did nothing to reduce the investment of American-owned companies in Mexican food production, there is little likelihood that irrigated agriculture will be curtailed in the near future. As a major employer of labour from the poorer rain-fed regions, the landowning classes in Mexico's irrigated regions try to ensure that little is done to threaten their supply of cheap labour. In 1976 President Echevarría surprised the country by supporting the demands of peasants in the irrigated north-west for more land. The effect of his support was to destabilize the Mexican presidency and reduce international 'confidence' in his administration. At the conclusion of his presidential term in 1982 his successor, Lopez Portillo, met an even greater economic crisis. Lopez Portillo's response was to draw on internal support through nationalist rhetoric. Mass demonstrations took place in Mexico City. But land was not invaded in the way it had been six years earlier. Instead, the international financial community came to Mexico's rescue. The tactics of the president paid off. It is extremely unlikely that land reform will be recommenced in the irrigated regions while Mexico faces a vast foreign debt like that of today.

The humid tropics

According to Cassio Luiselli, one of the architects of the SAM, Mexico's 'agricultural frontier', consists of more than 11 million ha of land which are suitable for agriculture but still remain unexploited (Luiselli 1979: 349). A more modest estimate, that of Mexico's Global Development Plan, refers to 3.3 million ha. Most of this land lies in the humid tropics, especially the states of Tamaulipas and Veracruz on the Gulf Coast. In these states, and others in the south and south-east of Mexico, land is often devoted to cattle-rearing rather than the production of basic grains. Some of this land was traditionally exploited by local peasant farmers on an irregular basis; it was 'held in reserve by maize-producing peasants' (Fernandez 1979). However, much of it is still jungle, although it is rapidly being depleted by cattlemen and companies interested in exploiting timber resources.

Since 1937 between 6 and 9 million ha of cattle land have been 'protected' from the agrarian reform process by decree of the President. Most of this land is in the drier north of the country, but the protection also extends to the more fertile tropical regions. Here, the *campesinos* are used as a cheap means of clearing the forest before being ejected by the wealthy ranchers. Although the humid tropics is relatively fertile livestock production is almost as extensive as in the arid and semi-arid north (Rutsch 1980). Moreover, extensive government funds have been funnelled into ranching, enabling the cattlemen to invest in more livestock, without improving stabling or animal hygiene. Cattle-raising is a speculative activity in the Mexican tropics, which provides easy gains at low cost, ties up large tracts of land, and makes wasteful use of natural resources. In areas such as the Huasteca, on the Gulf Coast and in Chiapas mounting violence between cattlemen and peasants is being met by new class and state strategies. Ranchers are seeking to legitimize their activities by converting a small part of their enormous empires to more intensive maize production.

In other parts of the Mexican tropics the state is playing an increasingly important role in managing unrest by direct intervention. *Ejidos* which were formerly undercapitalized are receiving large injections of funds, often as part of regional development projects such as Plan Chontalpa and the Papaloapan Basin (Barkin 1978; Ewell and Poleman 1980). The collective organization of production in these river basin projects gives the state a freer hand in managing resources and, until recently, was a factor in securing international funding. Such considerations often take precedence over employment-creation and help explain why small farm-systems research in tropical Mexico receives little official encouragement.

It is clear from what has been written that resource use in the humid tropics reflects the class interests of the locally powerful ranchers, together with government bureaucrats committed to managing land and water resources on a capital-intensive basis. Such practices effectively ignore the experience and participatory potential of poor peasant families. It is not clear that the abuse of power can be avoided while financial incentives exist to encourage the rapid conversion of virgin forest into extensive grazing land. Clearly, the classes which own and control natural resources in the humid tropics cannot be expected to favour alternative resource uses, as outlined in the SAM. Not surprisingly, the SAM policies failed to 'bite' in the humid tropical regions where they were, arguably, of greatest relevance.

THE POLITICS OF ENVIRONMENTAL POLICY

In this chapter we have analysed recent Mexican food and environmental policy, seeking to explain why policy changed in the way it did. We also considered the way that development policy is implemented in Mexico and the varying interpretations offered of the development process. Different ecological zones were identified with distinctive economic and social problems and conflicts.

In prescribing development policies we can lay no claim to 'objectivity'. Just as the development process is viewed differently by those of different ideological persuasions within Mexico, so outside observers exhibit biases of their own. For this reason it is often difficult for Mexicans to explain to North Americans why the 'problem' of illegal migration is not considered a 'problem' at all, south of the border. In Mexico itself it is United States' policy which is looked upon as problematical; whether it concerns private investment within Mexico, the treatment afforded Latin American migrants in the United States or the self-determination of Central American nations.

A serious appraisal of rural development policy involves examining the underlying objectives behind policies, as well as the formal arrangements to carry them out. Making better use of the natural environment implies benefits for some social classes rather than others; there is no such thing as optimal resource planning free from distributive implications. We also need to know which groups will be the agencies of environmental change, since shifts in resource use require political action on the part of beneficiaries or potential beneficiaries. Once we know who benefits, and who can be expected to exert pressure on behalf of environmental or food policies, we can re-examine the vexed question of policy implementation. These are the necessary steps in explaining how policy contributes to the development process, as well as how the development process itself helps to mould policy.

This chapter has been concerned with the way in which a specific policy, the Mexican Food System (SAM), was formulated and the effects of its introduction. The environmental crisis in rural Mexico exhibited two faces; one of them the poverty of neglected rain-fed regions, the other the commercial success, but economic dependency, of the irrigated regions. A policy which addressed rural poverty could only succeed by making fundamental changes in Mexico's structural position which were, ultimately, dependent on its relationship with the international economy, especially the United States. An increasingly important aspect of this international dimension is the way in which agricultural technologies can reduce the degree of control which social classes exercise over their environments. It is to this question that we turn in the next chapter.

6

Technology and the control of resources

In Chapter 2 we discussed the global distribution of natural resources in terms of the uses to which these resources were put. The depletion of resources and the degradation of much of the South's environment was attributed to a development model that put economic growth and the production of goods, before improved welfare and the eradication of poverty. Chapter 4 took up this theme from the specific standpoint of environmental poverty, and it was argued that although rural poverty was partly attributable to natural resource factors, the distribution of these resources reflected structural inequalities in society itself. A political economy approach to the environment needed to examine the interplay between specific resource endowments and structural processes, such as the market and public policy, which served to undermine the resource base.

The means adopted by mankind to change or influence the environment is the province of technology. 'Technology' is a very broad category, and distinguishable from the technical 'products' in which technology is embodied, which are transferred, in the physical sense, between groups of people in different countries (Evans and Adler 1979: 25). Technology is the application of scientific ideas to the environment, providing us with the knowledge 'by which we may be able to make ourselves masters and possessors of nature' (Descartes 1968: 78). If we take Descartes seriously, as we should, technology lies at the very heart of our relationship with nature.

Approaching technology from an environmentalist perspective requires a radical rethinking of the economic, demographic and biological elements in human survival. As Meadows commented, 'a whole culture has evolved around the principle of fighting against limits, rather than learning to live with them' (Meadows *et al.* 1972: 150). Technology is important not simply as the objective of man-made production, but as the mental equipment which translates ideas into action. Far from being apolitical, technology is always political; the means available to a society being structured around social values and interests as well as technical limitations. Once a technology exists, its use or non-use implies a political choice for, as one American philosopher recently observed, 'the act of not implementing a technology to modify a natural phenomenon is politically and morally different from the act of leaving nature alone' (Socolow 1976: 30–1). The interesting and important environmental questions about technology emerge not from specific cases of technological practice, but from the analysis of different technological options (Global 2000 1982: 271).

This brings us back to the debate which has run throughout previous chapters, between the orthodox Marxist position on development and that of radical ecology. Marxists have emphasized that the political consequences of technology are harmful if ownership and control are dictated by the interests of a dominant class (Sandbach 1980: 142). However, as the debate between protagonists of 'advanced' and 'appropriate' technologies has made clear, the social relations of production are indistinguishable from the technologies employed in production. This view is held by both 'sides' in the argument (Dickson 1974; Schumacher 1973; Emmanuel 1982). Later in this chapter it will be argued that technological changes in resource use imply shifts in the degree of control which different social classes exercise over their environment. Examples may be found in the 'Green Revolution', which followed the introduction of new varieties of high-yielding grains, and in the development of 'farming systems' around the small farmer's production situation. Furthermore, early indications are that the new biotechnologies are likely to be similarly distributive, both in terms of their social consequences and their political repercussions.

THE TECHNOLOGY OF FOOD SYSTEMS

Boserup argues that many of the differences between the developed and developing countries can be explained by the relationship between the technology employed in their food systems and the distribution of population. She distinguishes seven major food supply systems in low-technology countries. Each of these systems represents a different response to the problems of soil fertility, weeds, water control and erosion (Boserup 1981: 26). Historical parallels exist with present-day developed countries, in which annual cropping was substituted for short fallow periods in the transition to industrialized agriculture. Annual cropping demanded a higher labour input 'in order to plough, sow, plant and harvest the areas which had been left fallow under the old system or used as permanent pastures' (ibid.: 121).

According to Boserup, low-technology countries must either leave a considerable amount of land fallow or adopt labour-intensive agricultural practices. The first option only exists for countries with a sparsely settled population. In most poor countries the only alternative to intensive food cropping is intensive animal husbandry, and this implies heavy dependence on the production or importation of fodder. Unlike the developed countries, where widespread use of industrial chemicals reduces the need for fallowing, low-technology densely populated countries face very real limitations on the carrying capacity of their environments.

The existence of a plentiful supply of food from high-technology countries in North America and Western Europe poses additional problems for most countries in the South. The 'frontier societies' of North America and Australasia were opened up by European immigrants. These people combined extensive systems of food supply with high-level technology, by the standards of the time (Boserup 1981: 136). As a result their agricultures produced higher outputs per man hour than any other food producers prior to that date. In Western Europe, government intervention and the subsidized acquisition of capital by farmers enabled food stocks to grow equally dramatically in the period since the Second World War. Thus the balance was tipped in favour of the high-technology countries which, contrary to their experience during the Industrial Revolution, increased their exports of food to the poorer countries. These exports were maintained principally because the governments of the European Community countries and the United States wished to reduce the gap between the standard of living of the rural and urban populations within their own countries. The food surpluses that were dumped on the South were a direct effect of the northern governments' attempts to reduce sectoral imbalances at home.

Paradoxically, the effect on low-technology countries of having to absorb food imports served to worsen their own development situations. In those plantation societies where tropical products had been grown for the developed countries' markets, staple food production was undertaken through long-fallow methods. Cash-cropping, largely undertaken by men, was combined with food-cropping for subsistence, largely undertaken by women (ibid.: 147). These institutions grew up before the high-technology countries went into food surplus. The importation of food on favourable terms, from the United States and Western Europe, induced governments in the South to neglect investments in agriculture and rural infrastructure. As we saw in Chapter 2, agribusiness has been able to exploit food deficits in parts of Africa and Latin America by substituting technological control for the dependency created by 'comparative advantages' in trade. Boserup remarks acidly that 'If the food policy in . . . industrialised countries had encouraged food imports instead of subsidizing food exports, many Lower and Medium-Technology countries would no doubt have invested more in food production' (ibid.: 192).

The availability of relatively cheap imported food in the urban sectors of poorer countries influenced the distribution of investment in turn. Imported cheap food lowered relative wage costs in the cities and persuaded governments in low-technology countries to concentrate their attention on achieving industrialization. This, together with other forms of 'urban bias' promoted by development agencies, has been exhaustively reviewed by Lipton and others (Lipton 1977; Byres 1979). Whatever the merits of the 'urban bias' case as an explanation of rural underdevelopment, it is clear that the financial incentive to import food from high-technology countries exerted a hold on recent development policy in most parts of the South. By yielding to pressure from food donors, low-technology countries could prise more development aid out of them and concentrate both investment and taxation on the growing sector of export crops. The choices behind the adoption of technology in the food systems of both North and South have played an increasingly important role in closing doors as well as in opening them.

ADVANCED TECHNOLOGIES AND DEVELOPMENT

It is often asserted that technology has the capacity to transform society, sometimes in ways that are unsuspected. The converse is equally true, but rarely remarked upon. Society determines the way that technology is developed and employed. The full implications of this fact are observed very clearly in the way that technologies developed for use in one society create problems for other societies. Specifically, so-called 'advanced technology' as developed in the industrialized countries has contributed to underdevelopment in the poorer countries of the world.

The role of technology in underdevelopment is a complex issue, as Stewart (1977) demonstrates. If we begin by examining the characteristics of the technologies used in advanced industrial societies, it can quickly be appreciated that such technologies carry important development biases. First, advanced technology is very sensitive to even small changes in the end product. The marketed product is the outcome of a string of technical linkages. This means that 'in large part the technological package has to be accepted (or rejected) as a whole – part selection is impossible' (Stewart 1977: 58). Technology, then, is increasingly *indivisible* and its use therefore dependent on the transfer of complete technological packages.

Second, the trend towards the use of advanced technology is accentuated by 'selection mechanisms' in the less developed countries, which lead to factor prices favourable to this technology, giving entrepreneurs who use it greater control over the key resources of capital and labour (ibid.: 87). There is thus an inbuilt bias on the part of advanced technology that ensures a production environment conducive to its further development and adoption. This process has an ideological importance too. As Stewart argues, 'by reinforcing [the trend to advanced technology] the selection mechanisms appear to *justify* [its use] . . . making it appear privately and often socially profitable' (ibid.: 59). This is a good example of a theme to which this book makes constant reference; the institutionalization of certain resource uses so that they take on a legitimacy denied to alternative uses.

Third, advanced technology is developed together with an organizational form (large-scale industrial plant, marketing system and management practices), which are difficult to establish in many developing countries. The fact that technology is so closely associated with these organizational forms means that a country which employs the technology has, perforce, to employ the same organizational structure. Thus for several reasons technological transfer tends to lead to technological dependence, however ill-adapted the advanced technology is to the resource availabilities of the poorer country.

Fourth, advanced technology contributes to inequality as well as underdevelopment. At the sectoral level, the requirement for capital in the advanced technological sector tends to concentrate the poor countries' scarce capital resources in that sector to the neglect of the less developed sectors. Since labour productivity in the 'advanced' sector is higher, the adoption of rich-countries' technology tends to increase the difference in living standards between different social classes. The new products that are produced tend to replace, rather than supplement, existing products. Thus, 'while the transfer of inappropriate products requires inequality of income distribution if adequate markets are to be created, the transfer also contributes to the required inequality' (ibid.: 80).

Increased inequality is thus a necessary effect of advanced technology's use in developing countries. Again, the legitimizing function of technology can also be observed; increased income inequality, so necessary to the creation of a domestic market for advanced technology's goods, appears to justify the use of the technology itself. For the purposes of the national élite in the developing countries the technology is considered appropriate because it is necessary to their existence. By the same token the adoption of alternative technologies becomes increasingly difficult, because it requires redistributive policies that are politically unpalatable, and because the very 'success' of advanced technology tends to reduce the role of any technological alternatives. Social inequality is both the motor of a certain kind of technological advance and the outcome of the technological dependence to which this advance inevitably leads.

To appreciate the distortions in resource use that are implied by advanced technologies we should consider not only the effects of their introduction in developing countries, but also their development in certain sectors of developing countries, such as agriculture. In a stimulating article, Trigo, Pineiro and Fiorentino argue that the dominant theory of technological innovation advanced by neoclassical economists, 'induced innovation', does not prove adequate in explaining the case of Latin American agriculture. Induced innovation is the process whereby, in market economies, a set of institutional mechanisms derived from market relationships serve to bring about the type of technological development that is consistent with maximizing economic growth under existing resource endowments. Trigo and colleagues suggest that in Latin America 'inducement mechanisms . . . contribute to technological generation which is consistent with the factor endowments of the more powerful rural groups, which may differ from those of the majority of the farmers'. In other words, technological change in Latin America's agriculture follows lines that are dictated by private class interests, as mediated by the state and not only the imperatives dictated by the technology itself. Trigo and his colleagues are thus led to a provocative and radical conclusion from their survey of agricultural technology in Latin America. This is that:

> the uneven production and productivity increases of a number of different crops, under a wide variety of production conditions . . . can be explained on the basis of the social forces that characterize each of these production situations.
> (Trigo *et al.* 1979: 173)

It can be argued, of course, that the theory of 'induced innovation' is not incompatible with the Latin American case, if one adds the supplementary hypothesis that the more powerful rural groups gained this political ascendency from their superior factor endowments which enabled them to maximize economic growth to their advantage. Such an argument is logically consistent with the observations on social processes being advanced by Trigo and his colleagues, as it takes as its premise the existing distribution of factor endowments. The question of what groups derive benefits from this distributional system is thus put to one side.

TECHNOLOGICAL CONTROL

The Green Revolution

Between 1966 and 1970 new high-yielding varieties of wheat and rice were introduced to farmers throughout the less developed countries. These varieties, which had been developed at two principal international research centres, CIMMYT (Mexico) and IRRI (Philippines), produced dramatic increases in yields per acre, when used together with nitrogen-based fertilizers and controlled water systems. The 'Green Revolution' was born. The effects of the introduction of the new grain varieties have since been the subject of considerable debate amongst development agencies and writers (Griffin 1974; Farmer 1977; Pearse 1980; ILO 1977; Vallianatos 1976; Hewitt 1976; Lipton 1978; Leowontin 1979; Bowonder 1981; IDRC 1982).

It would be difficult to provide an adequate summary of the debate that has accompanied the 'Green Revolution', since the literature is vast and few of the 'Revolution's' effects are undisputed. The objective is, rather, to identify certain aspects of the transformation in the agricultures of large parts of Asia and some parts of Latin America, which have attracted attention. Within less than a decade large areas of monsoon Asia have been subjected to technological changes that have redistributed income and wealth, materially affected land tenure institutions, introduced new marketing arrangements, brought new nutritional patterns and disrupted the ecology of natural resources. Few technologies have had such widespread and radical effects. This discussion focuses on the way in which the Green Revolution altered the degree of control exercised over the environment by scientists, policymakers and commercial interests, and the implications for the environment of the social changes which the Green Revolution brought in its train.

The advantages of the Green Revolution were observed by the early 1970s. The new seed varieties brought higher yields per crop on the same area of land. In the case of rice they permitted shorter cropping cycles and thus enabled some farmers to make more economical use of their water resources. By enabling multiple cropping where previously only one crop had been cultivated, the new varieties helped the farmer economize on land. Under optimal conditions, using carefully controlled irrigation systems and the right mix of chemical fertilizers and insecticides, there was also an increase in labour employed on a unit of land. The technological 'package' was easily distributed, since it was as applicable to the fields of small farmers as to those of large farmers and did not require a major transformation of agricultural practices (Griffin 1974: 205). In this sense it was 'scale-neutral'. The Green Revolution was considered equitable by many protagonists largely because of this scale-neutrality, and because it was land displacing rather than labour displacing.

The chief disadvantages of the Green Revolution were equally apparent by the early 1970s. The new seed varieties were more delicate than those they replaced, less resistant to drought and flood, more vulnerable to plant diseases and infestation by insects. Substantial increases in yields were impossible without reliable irrigation and heavy doses of nitrogen-based fertilizers. The cost to the economy of utilizing the new varieties was high in terms of fixed and working capital (Griffin 1974: 209).

Nor were the effects of the Green Revolution as equitable as some assumed. Critics of the package pointed to what Pearse termed the 'talents effect' − those who had most to begin with gained most from the Green Revolution (Pearse 1980). Throughout Asia landlessness increased, as the new technology, combined with a population increase of 2.5 per cent per annum, compounded the effects of inequitable systems of land tenure and provided landlords with an incentive to dismiss their tenants (ILO 1977). The initial effect of increased employment tended to be offset by mechanization in some places, such as Uttar Pradesh in India. Larger farmers had better access to credit, and thus sources of inputs. Evidence accumulated that the food consumption of the poorest had dropped, especially of the coarse grains and pulses which formed a large part of the poor's diet (Bowonder 1981: 295). Similarly, those who had depended on fish from rivers and flooded fields as a source of protein were adversely affected by the polluting effects of increased chemical use and run-off (ibid.: 309). The pesticides used in conjunction with the new package were non-biodegradable and residues accumulated in fodder crops and milk, while soils suffered from a reduction in the humus layer, with consequent increases in erosion and desertification (Biswas and Biswas 1978).

Those who were in the best position to take advantage of the Green Revolution enjoyed 'not only high prices for their products, but also low prices for their inputs' (Griffin 1974: 211). Even sober reports from development agencies such as the Canadian IDRC concluded that:

It is evident that, where land distribution remains skewed, the direct effect of a technology that increases output per unit of land . . . will be to widen disparities in the absolute levels of family earnings from these crops.

(IDRC 1982: 33)

Although small and marginal farmers often benefited from the new package when they had access to the necessary inputs, the gap between large and small farmers has widened in almost every case studied. Lipton, a sympathetic observer of the new technology, conceded that 'the poorest producers – small farmers and landless labourers – got poorer relatively . . . "the system", therefore, has great power to alienate from poor producers even inputs well-suited to them' (Lipton 1978: 335). As we shall see, other commentators have placed emphasis on the need to work more closely with farmers for whom the Green Revolution technology is *not* well-suited.

The new seed varieties highlighted an aspect of agricultural research which has received more attention since the disadvantages of the Green Revolution became apparent. This is the relationship which obtains between agricultural research scientists in the national field station or international centre, and the farmers who are expected to benefit from technological change. The international research centres benefited from the increased flow of funds from development agencies, which was one consequence of the dramatic breakthroughs in genetic engineering. Some studies, like that of Vallianatos, which argues that technological transfer from the research station to the farmer was largely unsuccessful, seriously underestimated the degree to which technology was transferred (Vallianatos 1976: 148). It also confuses the question of how to make existing agricultural technology more socially useful, with the view that technology can be designed which can reduce social inequalities. These are related issues, but not reducible to the same thing. Studies of the effect of the Green Revolution in Mexico contribute to a similar confusion: it is implied that new wheat varieties were developed, rather than maize varieties, because of the political advantages that they would confer on large farmers and the attraction of this policy to the state (Hewitt 1976; Leowontin 1979). The possibility that biological break-throughs might lead to the setting of development priorities is more soundly based. In retrospect, one of the lessons of the Green Revolution is that social scientists were needed to make the requirements of research clearer *ex ante* (Lipton 1978: 335).

The Green Revolution has helped to precipitate at least two important debates concerning the application of technology to agriculture. The first of these debates concerns the distributional effects of the technological package; on incomes, nutrition, landholding and the political power of different classes in both rural and urban sectors. The second debate is more directly related to natural resources, and therefore relevant to the wider issue of technology's role in *altering the way* that social groups derive benefits from their environment, as well as the scale of those benefits. Briefly, the new high-yielding varieties enabled the natural environment to be closely controlled by supplying bought inputs (chemical fertilizers, insecticides, seeds and water). But this technical control over the environment was only exercised by the farmer in conjunction with extensionists, agricultural merchants and scientists. The farmer's control over the production system was, as a result, materially reduced. The growth of interest in farming systems research, which placed the farmer at the controls of the technological process, grew out of a recognition that the Green Revolution had brought most benefit to those who supplied the farmer, rather than the farmer or labourer himself. Farming systems research, by contrast, was intended to benefit those who employed their own resources on the farm. It involved *accommodating to* the environment, rather than controlling it.

Farming systems research

The interest in conducting research into farming systems was partly stimulated, as we have seen, by the social, economic and environmental effects of the Green Revolution. It would be a mistake, however, to think that the biological-engineering/technology-transference model adopted in the Green Revolution is strictly competitive with a farming systems approach. The first approach was orientated to producers of a single crop under irrigated conditions. In contrast, the farming systems approach takes as its focus small farmers who seek to maximize production of a range of crops, and livestock, under rain-fed conditions. The goal of the Green Revolution was to produce more staple food with which to feed more people, rural and urban. The goal of farming systems research is to improve the aggregate production of the small farmer and his family's welfare.

The reality which lies behind the farming systems approach was well expressed by Andrew Pearse in the following terms:

> Agricultural systems with a self-provisioning orientation should have a potentiality to provide the basis of a healthy, all-the-year round family diet. They cannot depend upon risky crops and high-cost inputs, or upon operations beyond the range of existing and teachable skills. Their capacity to provide work and a flow of cash for family members all the year round is important. At best their production gives rise to further economic activity in processing and transformation which can be carried on in the neighbourhood.   (1974: 49)

Some agricultural and social scientists were drawn to farming systems research by the positive lesson of the Green Revolution, 'that rural technology [was] a powerful tool for social engineering' (Chambers 1977: 350). Others regarded farming systems as an escape from the

biases of high technology and paternalism, stemming from a basic dissatisfaction with earlier research which was often inappropriate, in-
applicable and implied heavy risks for small farmers (Norman 1972;
ICRISAT 1980). The discovery that peasant farmers operated their own
'research systems', selecting appropriate technologies or adapting those
that were available to them, has produced some of the most interesting
contributions to the farming systems canon (Biggs and Clay 1981;
Mooney 1979; Bull 1982). One project in which this discovery led to a
considerable commitment on the part of some of the project staff was
Plan Puebla, a programme to disseminate information on maize technology (Redclift 1983). Until farming systems research was fully understood and acted upon, the situation described by Biggs would continue
to be common:

> Only too often [scientists and extension agents], instead of monitoring
> the creative way in which farmers have modified and adapted inappro-
> priate 'packages of practices' and then capitalising on such new
> developments by passing the information on to extension agents, have
> seen the non-adoption of the full package as a sign of backwardness on
> the part of farmers or as a result of inadequacies in pricing policy, the
> supply of inputs etc.
>   (1981: 10)

The contrast with farming systems work at its purest is very clear.
Collinson, one of the most inspired educators employing the farming
systems model, argues that 'the challenge lies in the circumstances of
smallholder agricultural sectors and the characteristics of small farmers'
(1979: 2). Understanding why such farmers adopt technological practices, or reject them, is a first principle of this approach. The farming
system exists prior to any useful research input; 'farmers operate farming systems, they don't *adopt* them' (ibid.: 7).

The principles behind farming systems research are simple. First,
every attempt is made to economize on the use of non-farm inputs, such
as paid labour, chemical fertilizers and seeds. Second, every attempt is
made to maximize the use of what small farmers have relatively abun-
dantly, such as family labour and organic fertilizers. The farmers' risk
avoidance strategies are taken to heart by the agronomists who work with
them, and the threats to the fragility of their system understood. At its
most generous farming systems research includes three implicit assumptions. These are that man and nature are both part of the same system;
that the system is considered to include areas distant from the location, if
those areas are affected by production processes (such as erosion silting
up reservoirs); and that the time scale in which analysis is undertaken
must be long enough to enable the effects of ecological processes to be

seen (Avery, Schramn and Shapiro 1978). In practice, such an ambitious definition is not workable, and most farming-systems research is more narrowly circumscribed. The essential ingredient is that the farmer's behaviour is understood as logical and agricultural research goes more than half-way to meet him.

Farming systems research can be either 'upstream' (that is, originating in the research station and encompassing the farmer) or 'downstream' (that is, originating on the farmer's fields and encompassing the research station). It begins with the classification of the farming system, but moves on through other stages: the diagnosis of constraints and opportunities for future intervention, the generation of recommendations to be tried out on farmers' fields, the implementation of ideas and their evaluation (Maxwell 1983). Ideally, the research team working with the farmer is interdisciplinary, but 'specialists do not cease to exist, rather they bring their expertise to bear on problem-solving in a complementary and cooperative fashion' (Gostyla and White 1979: 5).

One of the principal problems in winning converts to farming systems research from the agricultural and social science disciplines is that multidisciplinary, farm-based research requires a new mentality. Professional credit and financial resources are largely found in commodity-based programmes and the laboratory, rather than in working with farmers on their fields. Targeted, multidisciplinary research can only be undertaken out of conviction, and the resources or political will necessary to establish the new approach are not always forthcoming. It is the view of some commentators that this approach, by concentrating on small farmers and operating at low cost is 'less susceptible by far to distortion, corruption and the talents effect, than measures which rely directly on administrative or political support' (Chambers 1977: 349). However, it also requires high levels of commitment amongst agricultural research staff, extension workers and others.

Farming systems research is time-consuming for the scientist, especially if 'the farmer has . . . enough control of the experiment to enable him to make an independent evaluation of the technology' (Gostyla and Whyte 1979: 46). Collinson argues that a balance has to be sought between the understanding of local farming systems and the farmers' participation in experiments. He sees experimentation with farmer involvement as a possible substitute for *ex ante* research into farming systems (1979: 11). The possibilities opened by farming systems are almost limitless, and the deployment of scarce agricultural research staff to the understanding of complex farming systems can be costly. In this sense it may be inevitable that the complexity of cropping systems lies with the farmers, rather than the agricultural research station (Jodha 1979: 19). Many of the benefits derived from work with farming systems have been circumstantial and indirect; the experience of multidisciplinary research, the re-examination of research undertaken at the field station or in farm 'trials'. The importance of social and ecological constraints in the behaviour of small farmers, and the evolution of their own processes of research and development, have proved to be of importance for other types of agricultural and rural development programme. In the next section the implications of putting resource use for industrial growth before greater equity are illustrated by considering Brazil's celebrated industrial alcohol programme.

ENERGY VERSUS FOOD: BRAZIL'S ETHANOL PROGRAMME

The 'successes' of the Green Revolution were dependent on increasing inputs of fertilizers, most of which were partially derived from petroleum sources. This placed a heavy burden on poor countries, such as India, which needed to import the bulk of their oil. Increasing use of tractors, and mechanical transport in general, also absorbs expensive petroleum that is ultimately in limited supply. The cost to the poor farmer of heavy dependence on petroleum and chemical-based fertilizers and herbicides is prohibitive. These factors taken together help account for the appeal of a farming systems approach especially in oil-deficient developing countries.

The energy crisis affecting the semi-developed countries is no less severe than that facing countries like India, and the poverty of the masses in these countries is not ameliorated by the higher level of industrialization. Brazil is a case in point. Brazil's dependence on imported sources of energy is a direct result of the development path it has followed for the last three decades. In 1940, 80 per cent of Brazil's energy consumption was derived from the biomass, principally firewood. Only 15 per cent came from hydroelectricity. In 1980, electricity represented over a quarter of the total and the biomass had been replaced by petroleum (Cardoso 1980: 114) (see *Table 4*). The modernization of Brazil's energy sector, made necessary by rapid industrialization and urbanization, exacerbated the country's external dependence. Domestically, the development model placed emphasis on the rapid diffusion of consumer durables, the concentration of income and regional inequality, all of which were made possible by oil imports. Brazil's dependence on the internal combustion engine cost it eleven billion US dollars in 1980 (Saint 1982: 223).

The principal factor in Brazil's energy dependence, then, is its heavy reliance on motor transport, for private and commercial purposes. It has

Table 4 Brazil: primary energy consumption (in percentages)

	Petroleum	Coal	Hydroelectric	Biomass
1970	38.3	3.9	18.9	38.9
1975	43.9	3.2	23.7	29.2
1977	42.2	4.0	26.1	26.6
1978	43.0	4.4	25.6	27.0
1979	41.1	4.3	28.3	26.3
1980*	41.2	4.6	28.4	25.8

* estimated

In 1980, of the 25.8% of energy derived from the biomass, 7% was attributable to the alcohol programmes, 16.4% to fuel wood and 2.4% to charcoal.

Source: Van der Pluijin 1982: 87.

been calculated that in 1978, 96 per cent of passengers and 70 per cent of freight were transported by road (Cardoso 1980: 115). Although Brazil has an important hydroelectricity programme, liquid hydrocarbons, derived from petroleum and coal, are only partially replaceable by electricity, and only for industrial consumption. Transport, rather than manufacturing industry, takes the lion's share of energy consumption in Brazil. There is every indication that without a radical shift in energy policy, Brazil's consumption of petroleum would continue to increase.

In view of the country's commitment to its present development model, with the implied increase in dependence on imported energy sources, the military government has been forced to introduce new policies since 1979. These policies were designed to restrict the consumption of petroleum and replace it with alcohol derived from the biomass. Brazil's National Alcohol Programme had been initiated four years earlier, but worsening trade conditions accelerated the introduction of new policy measures. It has rapidly become one of the most disputed programmes to emerge from the biotechnology revolution. The alcohol programme, with a budget of over five billion US dollars, is designed to stimulate ethyl alcohol (ethanol) production based largely on the use of sugar cane and cassava as feedstocks. The plan envisages a major substitution of alcohol for gasoline, accounting for three-quarters of all liquid combustible fuel by the year 2000 (Saint 1982: 223). Liquid fuel production from energy crops promises to be increasingly important for other countries with similar resource advantages for energy farming, severely limited fossil fuel supplies and a balance of payments situation distorted by petroleum imports. As we shall see, biotechnology's potential is intimately linked with decisions about social priorities in food, energy and waste disposal policies.

The environmental implications of Brazil's alcohol programme are serious enough to warrant close attention. They are, as we shall see, inevitably distributive in their consequences and, as such, illustrate the way in which technology enables different social classes to derive very unequal benefits from resource conversion. Among the most important effects of the alcohol programme the following can be identified: the progressive neglect of staple food crops and domestic food supply, the increased concentration of land, and worsening regional inequality.

The decision to stimulate sugar cane production in Brazil is of immediate benefit to the 250 plantation-owning families who control two-thirds of sugar production and the entire processing industry (Saint 1982: 224). Based on the experience of existing irrigated plantations, plans have been drawn up to develop 750,000 ha of irrigated cane for alcohol production within the watershed of the Sao Francisco River valley where yields are high and unit costs particularly low. Such projects rely heavily on seasonal wage labour and serve to increase the importance of Sao Paulo at the expense of states in the poor north-east, where sugar production is less cost efficient (Van der Pluijin 1982).

The decision to concentrate on increasing sugar production was made after considering the possibilities offered by cassava production for alcohol. Brazil is the world's largest producer of cassava which, unlike sugar cane, grows well under a variety of agroclimatic conditions. It is grown largely by resource-poor farmers on small plots of land, throughout the year. As is so often the case with crops grown by peasant farmers, cassava has received little research funding and has been systematically neglected in credit and extension programmes (Saint 1982: 226). If existing technology to increase cassava yields were employed, it would become roughly competitive with sugar cane in terms of alcohol production.

In addition to the possibilities raised by a cassava-based alcohol programme, the development of ethanol from sugar cane is likely to contribute further to land concentration in Brazil. The available evidence suggests that between 1974 and 1979 the new 362,000 ha of land devoted to cane were cultivated largely at the expense of food crops. Corn and rice declined in cultivated areas by 35 per cent in these years. At the same time, the price of food staples rose dramatically in the cities. As Saint argues:

In a country where an advantaged 20 per cent of the population owns almost 90 per cent of the automobiles and a disadvantaged 50 per cent spends at least half their income on food, the policy decision ... comes perilously close to choosing between allocating calories to cars or to people.
(1982: 230)

Even commentators whose sympathy lies with the sugar ethanol programme admit that the intended increase in acreage devoted to sugar is likely to have a negative impact on the production and availability of food, as well as personal income distribution (Van der Pluijin 1982: 92).

The specifically environmental consequences of the ethanol programme are more disputed. Cardoso notes that the production of sugar cane alcohol generates an extremely polluting by-product which is currently responsible for considerable river pollution (Cardoso 1980: 119). On the other hand, alcohol contributes less to air pollution than petroleum fumes, largely because its vapours do not contain carbon monoxide or lead. Interestingly, the industrial waste from alcohol production can be used as a fertilizer, and becomes cost-effective if small distilleries are substituted for large ones. However, this option has not been given the attention it deserves by the Brazilian government (Saint 1982: 233).

The issues raised by Brazil's ethanol programme should not be restricted to the economic efficiency of the programme as a means of saving foreign exchange (Barzelay and Pearson 1982: 144). As Cardoso remarks, the basic choices must not be limited to the analysis of technological substitutes, important as these may be, for the underlying issues concern '*who* consumes energy and *for what purpose*' (Cardoso 1980: 119). There has been very little questioning of the opportunity costs of the ethanol programme, both in terms of a social assessment of its effects and in terms of the need for an energy *conservation* policy, rather than an energy substitution policy. Again, the issue of technological control of the environment is paramount, since the ethanol programme serves both to marginalize further many poor food-crop producers, and to concentrate more power in the hands of those who own and control the new technology.

ADVANCED OR APPROPRIATE TECHNOLOGY?

The effects of so-called 'advanced' technology have been reviewed in some detail in this chapter, without considering the alternative posed by 'appropriate' technology. Schumacher, in *Small is Beautiful* (1973), framed four propositions which facilitated the choice of technology in developing countries. First, he suggested that technology should enable workshops to be located where people lived. Second, he argued that technology must enable a large number of jobs to be created without calling for an unattainable level of capital formation or imports. Third, the production methods employed should be relatively simple, so that difficult skills are minimized in production, marketing, raw material supply and finance. Finally, he argued that production should be with local materials and for local use. The emphasis in the argument for appropriate technology lies in minimizing the investment in productive capacity, while making maximum use of the resource which is most freely available – labour (Evans and Adler 1979).

The view that appropriate technology provides some of the answers to the problem of underdevelopment has recently been challenged, in a provocative way, by Emmanuel. Emmanuel believes that in general the most advanced and capital-intensive technology is also the technology which maximizes output, and is most beneficial to developing countries. He also argues that the multinational companies are the best instruments for transferring advanced technology to the developing world.

Emmanuel asserts that seeking appropriate technology is misconceived, since 'a technology that was made to measure for poor countries would be a poor technology' (1982: 104). The only route to genuine autonomy and greater independence for countries of the South is by acquiring the same technology as the most developed countries. He sees the less developed countries simply as less developed capitalist countries, ignoring the possibility that development might occur in a non-capitalist form. This leads him to a form of technological determinism, in that 'advances' in technology bring about 'advances' in culture:

> In the final analysis, one therefore has the culture corresponding to one's technology and it is quite illusory to seek the technology corresponding to one's culture. ... Capitalism by its very nature ... develops productive forces, and if this development does not, *ipso facto*, lead to the satisfaction of 'social needs', it nonetheless constitutes, via the political struggles made possible by a certain pluralism inherent in the higher phase of the industrial revolution, a much more favourable framework for a certain satisfaction of these needs than those of past class regimes.
>
> (ibid.: 104–5)

Emmanuel's contribution to the debate about 'appropriate technology' is important. Too often the advocates of this approach make a simplistic comparison between production for 'social needs' and production for 'profit', as if the two were necessarily incompatible. Capitalism in the West has raised general living standards considerably while leaving massive inequalities between social classes. The question is whether, given the social costs implicit in capitalist development, the economic motor itself can produce the effects in the developing countries that have already been experienced in the developed. Technology that is 'small-scale' may thus be more 'appropriate' in certain circumstances, but without conferring the development potential of larger-scale technology.

By the same token, the adoption of 'advanced' technology does not ensure development on the lines of the industrialized countries.

At a more pragmatic level Emmanuel is misguided in believing that rapidly industrializing countries, such as Japan, South Korea and Taiwan, owe their development to the wholesale adoption of advanced technology. These countries have acquired their technology at arms length, breaking down the technological package they were offered, separating the acquisition of technology from finance and the ownership of resources. In this way they 'have managed to get the best out of the technology, without suffering its worst effects' (Stewart 1983: 23). As Frances Stewart has written, the argument for appropriate technology is not that jobs should be put before output, but that techniques can be developed which promote both.

The effects of concentrating ownership in new technologies within the developed countries can be illustrated by reference to the burgeoning microelectronics industries which have been established in some Asian countries. King concludes that 'at quite an early stage, the silicon chip will transform most of the existing electronic products and render unnecessary much of the delicate assembly work which has proved so beneficial to countries such as Korea, Taiwan and Hong Kong (1980: 109). The new technologies are increasingly information storage systems, their ownership and control conferring political advantages on transnational companies based in the North. The countries of the North are seeking to maximize the benefits of these technologies by restructuring their own productive and service industries (Rada 1981: 43). Moreover, the facility to forecast new technological breakthroughs is confined to the North, where an increase in this capacity is urgently sought by existing commercial and government interests.

BIOTECHNOLOGY AND THE ENVIRONMENT

Biotechnology has been defined as 'the application of biological organisms, systems or processes to manufacturing and service industries' (Smith 1981: 1). Essentially, biotechnology enables natural substances, available in the biomass, to be transformed at low energy cost and on a large scale, into a variety of materials for use in food production, alternative energy sources, waste recycling and pharmaceutics. It is no exaggeration to say that biotechnology has the potential to revolutionize man's relationship with the natural environment.

The possibilities opened by genetic engineering and suitable enzyme systems are such that almost any definition of what constitutes natural resources today will need to be revised in the light of biotechnological advances. Biotechnology uses very little fossil fuel and promises to assist in the development of alternative energy sources. By replacing petrochemical feedstocks, biotechnological advances should reduce the dependence on bought inputs which, as we have seen, the Green Revolution fostered. The search for protein, which has led to the conversion of crop land for forage and the extension of ranching, could similarly be revolutionized through advanced biotechnological processes. Already proteins may be extracted from liquid wastes by ultrafiltration, and the use of microbes as protein producers has proved successful experimentally. The field of study known as single cell protein production, or SCP, will radically alter the way we derive foodstuffs and the food systems to which they give rise.

Waste recycling is another area which is ripe for biotechnological advances. Indeed, it has been claimed that 'the primary objectives of biotechnology are to improve the management and utilization of the vast volumes of waste organic materials to be found throughout the world' (ibid.: 9). The biomass resources that are available in nature, particularly in tropical and subtropical regions, are so rich when linked to biotechnological processes that they might even precipitate a shift in the global balance of economic power. We have already considered some of the negative impacts of biotechnology as evidenced in Brazil's ethanol programme. Biomass production promises to attract new capital into agriculture, inducing new developments in the capital goods sector (distilleries, bioreactors) and technological innovation in distilling, the use of residues and pollution control.

In the future, increasing cross-penetration between the chemical and food industries is likely to be related to shifts in the circuit from research through technology to industrial production, in which transnational companies and the national state both seek to play a major part. The relationship between foreign and national capital within countries of the South, and the mediating and initiating role of the state, are likely to change in response to these technological breakthroughs. To give one illustration of this, food production can either follow current trends, in which the dynamic sector of the food industry is associated with more sophisticated foods, such as dairy products, cheeses and wines, for which industrially-produced enzyme technology is well established. Or it can concentrate on low-cost sources of protein for food programmes at the other end of the market, such as using soya-based meat and milk substitutes, where these are available. Decisions about the distributive consequences of biotechnology development hang, like other aspects of environmental policy, on the socially constructed definition of priorities and needs. At the moment it is difficult to predict the direction that changes will take. However, it is becoming increasingly clear that any discussion of development and the environment will need to take cognizance of biological resource conversion as well as natural resource endowments.

Until recently it was possible to analyse the role of technology in natural resource use by reference to the ownership of technology and its location. Small farmers employed hoe or plough technologies; large farmers employed tractors or combine harvesters. As we have seen in this chapter, such an approach is inadequate today. Farmers are on the receiving end of technological 'packages', composed of chemical inputs and genetic materials, such as seeds. Agricultural production makes use of the natural environment by interfering radically with the way it is organized: spraying crops from the air, breeding disease-resistant strains, controlling water supplies through irrigation infrastructure. Equally importantly, 'technological packages' are linked to the supply of components and the marketing of produce, as well as research and development systems. The farmer, large or small, may or may not 'own' the land he works, but he is unlikely to own the technology he employs on it. Increasingly, in fact, he does not own the technology himself but subscribes to its use through contractual arrangements with agribusiness firms or governments. The expertise in modifying agricultural technologies lies, not with the farmer, but with the government advisory service or multinational company which provides advice. In this process ownership becomes separated from control, and 'ownership' itself becomes a problematical concept.

This chapter has discussed the process through which technological control assumes more importance than formerly, in societies where the ownership of land or water resources determines their use. Clearly, land tenure practices and labour processes do not change overnight; nor does the ownership of natural resources cease to be important. The essential point is that, increasingly, technological control of the production process replaces the physical coercion associated with colonization and the North's control of trading relations. Social control is exercised through access to, and use of, technology rather than land tenure or labour processes *per se*. The social relations of production are modified in line with technological changes. Social control does not disappear, but it is mediated in different ways.

The interest of biotechnology lies precisely in the way it promises to separate technology not only from traditional concepts of 'ownership' but also from dependence upon a fixed concept of 'value'. Agricultural technology is no longer developed for different environments but for combinations of biological resources. Resources assume a value which they did not previously possess. The question that arises is not whether technology should be developed which is 'appropriate' to a given environment, but whether reducing dependence on the natural environment necessarily brings benefits to those whose natural environment is impoverished, or whose poverty locates them at the margins of natural abundance. Biotechnology is today a term for genetic engineering; in the future it might be seen as a euphemism for social engineering.

7

Development and the environment: a converging discourse?

It may be said that political economy has produced its own antithesis in the movement for conservation. At the same time the structural processes undermining the environment are frequently ignored in favour of less 'political' explanations of poverty and dependency in the South. Environmentalism lacks a coherent political direction. The central paradox considered in this book is that while development threatens the environment in very tangible ways, we are left without the moral or intellectual equipment to meet the challenge. Or are we? This chapter examines some of the ways in which the development and environmental discourses are currently being conducted, and suggests a number of new directions which these discourses could take.

DIVERGENT DISCOURSES: OBJECTIONS TO POLITICAL ECONOMY

In the opening chapter it was suggested that some of the difficulties faced by political economy in incorporating an environmentalist perspective stemmed from the assumptions of economic growth under capitalism which were carried over into the socialist project, as conceived by Marx. Man's mastery of nature, rather than placing limits on material advance, was actually a necessary precondition for that advance. Although Marx saw labour as a commodity under capitalism and its alienation as necessary to the development of a socialist consciousness, nature was not afforded the same attention. Man acted upon nature in constructing the material world. Nature was passive.

The objections to political economy currently being voiced take issue with a number of central tenets in Marxism. As we saw in Chapter 3, Rudolf Bahro has argued for a more critical position on commodity production. In his view commodity production is not a necessary condition of human existence, but the developed countries' obsession with commodities does deflect attention from the full implications of its economic model (Bahro 1982a). André Gorz argues with similar

Barbira-Scazzochio, F. (ed) (1980) *Land, People and Planning in Contemporary Amazonia*, Cambridge Centre of Latin American Studies, University of Cambridge Occasional Publication No. 3.

Barkin, D. (1978) *Desarollo regional y reorganización campesina*, Mexico City, Nueva Imagen.

Barkin, D. (1981) *The Use of Agricultural Land in Mexico*, Working Papers in US–Mexican Studies no. 17, San Diego, University of California.

Barnes, B. and Edge, D. (eds) (1982) *Science in Context: readings in the sociology of science*, Milton Keynes, Open University Press.

Barraclough, S. (1973) *Agrarian Structure in Latin America*, Massachusetts, D. C. Heath.

Barraclough, S. and Domike, A. (1970) 'Agrarian Structure in Seven Latin American Countries', in *Agrarian Problems and Peasant Movements in Latin America*, New York, Anchor Doubleday.

Bartra, A. (1976) 'Colectivización o proletarización: el caso del Plan Chontalpa', *Cuadernos Agrarios*, 1 (4).

Bartra, R. (1974) *Estructura agraria y clases sociales en México*, Mexico City, Serie Popular Era.

Barzelay, M. and Pearson, S. R. (1982) 'The Efficiency of Producing Alcohol for Energy in Brazil', *Economic Development and Cultural Change*, 31 (1).

Bauer, P. T. (1981) *Equality, the Third World and Economic Delusion*, London, Methuen.

Bauer, P. T. and Yamey, B. S. (1957) *The Economics of Underdeveloped Countries*, Cambridge, Cambridge University Press.

Bell, C. (1974) 'Ideology and Economic Interests in Indian Land Reform', in Lehmann, D. (ed.) *Agrarian Reform and Agrarian Reformism*, London, Faber.

Bergmann, T. (1977) *The Development Models of India, the Soviet Union and China*, Assen, Van Gorcum.

Bernstein, H. (ed.) (1973) *Underdevelopment and Development*, Harmondsworth, Penguin.

Bernstein, H. (1977) 'Notes on Capital and Peasantry', *Review of African Political Economy*, 10, 60–73.

Bernstein, H. (1979) 'African Peasantries: a theoretical framework', *The Journal of Peasant Studies*, 6 (4).

Beteille, A. (1974) *Studies in Agrarian Social Structure*, Oxford, Oxford University Press.

Biggs, S. (1981) 'Monitoring for Re-planning Purposes: the role of research and development in river basin development', in Saha, S. K. and Barrow, C. (eds) *River Basin Planning: theory and practice*, Chichester, John Wiley.

of nature did not reduce his dependence upon it; rather, it induced feelings of anxiety and guilt. The very passivity of nature in the face of its destruction caused alarm. To radical ecologists the only solution is to reject the 'scientific world view' from which 'we have constructed a deficient code for reading nature' (Skolimowski 1981: vii). This might even involve the exhortation to pursue a more spiritual version of ecology, a kind of pantheism, in which we take our moral as well as practical cues from the environment (Riddell 1981). Such views do not have wide currency, however, and remain isolated from both political activity and a popular social base.

The development discourse is usually conducted through comparing the claims of neoclassical economics and Marxist political economy. However, both approaches have been found wanting, notably in their inability to provide an alternative to industrial society. The growth of interest in our responsibilities to nature, in alternatives to alienated labour and commodity fetishism, and the attention which feminists have paid to the social construction of gender, should give us cause to reflect on the trajectory which 'development' has taken in industrial society. These perspectives are potentially elements in a new discourse about development, which is more holistic, concentrates on sustainable resource use and identifies the satisfaction of human needs through mechanisms other than the market economy.

WIDENING THE DISCOURSE

The case for a more catholic approach to environmental issues does not rest solely with the limitations of political economy. Increasingly, movements and ideas are crossing the boundaries in which discourse is usually conducted. Amongst some feminists the search for a coherent version of both socialist and feminist traditions has brought to attention the role of women and class in early industrial history (Taylor 1983). The bonding of feminism and ecology has been pursued with even more determination, to the point where it constitutes an element in the divisions within the feminist movement.

The link between ecology and feminism has been the subject of some debate. Some writers see the association of women and nature as 'the source of a natural kinship between feminism and ecology' (Capra 1981: 15). The women's movement has produced varying responses, however. To those feminists who are convinced of 'the feminine principle', the essentially *different* contribution of women to civilization and culture, the fusion of ecology and feminism is inevitable:

Ecology is universally defined as the study of the balance and interrelationship of all life on Earth. The motivating force behind feminism

is the expression of the feminine principle. As the essential impulse of the feminine principle is the striving towards balance and inter-relationship, it follows that feminism and ecology are inextricably interconnected.
(Leland 1981: 33)

Susan Griffin's prose poem (1980) is inspired by the same purpose. The most eloquent version of this position is that of Carolyn Merchant, whose book *The Death of Nature* linked the subordination of nature to that of women, and located the process in the scientific revolution of early modern Europe. The central tenet of Merchant's book is that the scientific revolution reversed 'ecological' ways of thinking. Thus:

in investigating the roots of our current environmental dilemma and its connections to science, technology and the economy, we must re-examine the formation of a world view and a science that, by reconcep-tualizing reality as a machine, rather than a living organism, sanctioned the domination of both nature and women.   (Merchant 1980: xvii)

Not all feminists are convinced of the unity of interest between the ecology and women's movements. Some deplore the connection, and see it as a regression which is bound to reinforce sex-role stereotyping. This fear is partly a response to those feminists, such as Mary Daly and Susan Griffin, who believe 'that women should identify with nature against men' and who object that 'the socialist feminist solution has been to align women with culture in culture's struggle with nature' (King 1981: 13). On the other hand, the linking of ecology and feminism is seen by their protagonists as weakening the women's movement rather than giving it strength, in spite of the evidence from West European 'Green' move-ments that resistance to nuclear rearmament calls for a response that women are particularly, if not uniquely, able to make. The link between resistance to nuclear rearmament, feminism and environmental action has been given tangible form in the Green politics emerging throughout Western Europe.

The concern with practical ways of opposing the direction taken by industrial society is also producing an historical re-evaluation of the link between socialism and the environment. As Merchant suggests, 'new social concerns generate new intellectual and historical problems' (1980: xvi). Raymond Williams, in a characteristically thought-provoking essay, has traced the divergencies between socialism and ecology to the period, around the middle of the nineteenth century, when 'there was a tendency . . . to say that the central problem of modern society was poverty, and that the solution to poverty was production, and more production' (1981: 6). This observation was at odds with what Williams regards as the essential socialist case, which rests on the *co-existence* of wealth and poverty, order and disorder, production and waste. In Williams' view the connectedness of industrial society's 'successes', including economic growth, with industrial society's 'failures', including environmental depredation, lies at the heart of the socialist critique (ibid: 8).

However much one may sympathize with what Williams is saying, including the revitalization of popular crafts with which the name of William Morris is associated, the socialist project does not *inevitably* make reference to the environment. Raymond Williams sees 'the problem of resources' as the key to world capitalism's crisis, and the threat to world peace (ibid.: 18). A more orthodox socialist view, such as that of Sutcliffe, dedicated to examining the nature of the world capitalist crisis, makes no reference to natural resources or the environment, with the implication that such problems, if they exist at all, can be addressed solely through altering the ownership of production (Sutcliffe 1983: 14). The battle to get people to consider the environment as a political issue in development needs to be waged not only outside the socialist movement, but *within* it. Pointers exist in the identification of food politics presented in a companion volume to that of Sutcliffe (Clutterbuck and Lang 1982).

Another perspective on the environment which is not dismissive or doctrinaire, but which stays closer to the socialist tradition, is that represented by libertarian environmentalism and anarchism (Bookchin 1980). This perspective has recently been enlarged by attempts to develop an intellectual framework which could provide the basis for a future society organized on 'ecological principles' (Capra 1981). The disenchantment with the modern world which found expression in a variety of 'alternative' perspectives, from Marcuse's updated borrowings from the Frankfurt School, to Illich's questioning of the 'institutionalization of values' has a momentum that is not determined by orthodoxies of Right or Left. The interest in utopian radicalism and voluntaristic 'intentional' communities did not depart with the 1960s, and shows evidence of surfacing again in the work of radical planners and urbanists (see Friedmann's chapter in Redclift and Mingione 1984). Utopianism, once a derided concept, has flowered on both sides of the Atlantic as a continuing part of the sociological tradition founded by Tonnies, Weber and other nineteenth-century critics of industrial society (Kumar 1978; Jones 1983).

REDIRECTING THE DISCOURSE

The environmentalism of the 1960s and early 1970s was very largely a product of prosperity. The debate about the 'quality of life' assumed importance in North America and parts of Western Europe just as the problems associated with the physical creation of goods seemed to have been solved. The environmental crisis was largely subjective for most of those drawn into the environmental movement. Those who *experienced* the effects of resource degradation were living at the margins of their society in the South.

The 1980s changed all that. Economic recession in the industrialized North has led to mass unemployment together with rearmament, and widespread political disaffection among certain social groups: especially women, ethnic minorities and the young. Such disaffection existed in the 1960s, of course, culminating in the events of May 1968 in Paris. However, one has only to see a film of the period, such as Jean-Luc Godard's *La Chinoise*, to appreciate the gulf that separates the Maoist students of the 1960s from the unemployed youth of today. Today the promise of economic growth is not derided by the Left because of its hidden dangers; it is simply disbelieved. The argument being waged for more growth is being waged in the face of a severe and lasting recession. It is largely a glint in the eye of politicians.

Where does this leave the environmental movement? On the one hand, the scale of unemployment in the industrialized countries seems to have led the faltering international economy into a desperate attempt to recover economic growth. On the other hand, social deprivation cannot easily be translated into environmental action. It is clear that in the developed countries, as well as the underdeveloped, those who are most materially affected by the environmental crisis are least likely to wage a successful political struggle. For those with a major stake in their society the promise of future economic growth is real enough; for those who are divorced from material prosperity such promises take on the character of hollow rhetoric.

In Chapter 3 it was argued that environmentalism existed in 'radical' and 'conservative' versions. The problems of the radical version were identified as stemming from the absence of an agency, such as the proletariat in Marxist theory, capable of bringing about the desired social order. The division of labour within capitalist society makes general agreement about environmental issues elusive, since different groups and classes stand to benefit in different ways from the existing social order. Thus radical ecology is forced to prescribe a programme that can only work within a radical ecological society. Anything less than a cultural sea-change leads to frustration and apathy.

An illustration of the problems faced by more conservative groups is outlined by Lowe and Goyder in their recent book. The European Environmental Bureau, a forum for environmental pressure groups throughout the Common Market, is constantly poised between its commitment to maintain the environmental principles of its supporters, and the need to enter into a style of advocacy, 'reasoned and moderate argument rather than open confrontation' favoured by the European Economic Community institutions (Lowe and Goyder 1983: 171). Within the EEC multilateral action has considerable advantages over action by individual countries, but the stultifying effects of the European bureaucracy and the inability of environmental groups to impose sanctions against disputed policies are ultimately frustrating, even for those groups which favour a more conciliatory stance.

A leading pointer to the failure of conservative environmentalism is the role and activities of the United Nations Environmental Programme (UNEP). This has been succinctly expressed in a recent paper:

> the Stockholm Conference envisaged an institutional initiative that would foster system-wide endeavour on environmental matters: in other words, an Environmental Program of the United Nations. Instead, we got a United Nations Environment Program – a different kind of creature altogether, with capacities more narrowly conceived and with resources in short supply. (Myers and Myers 1982: 201)

UNEP's role has been widely misunderstood. It is not a United Nations executive agency, empowered to carry out its own programmes. It is not a sprawling organization comparable to the World Health Organization (WHO) or the International Labour Office (ILO), with a huge staff and massive budget. Most importantly, it cannot be *responsible* for the world environment, most of which lies inside the boundaries of sovereign nations, which resent any interference from the UN. Its role is entirely 'catalytic', designed to co-ordinate the environmental activities of larger UN agencies and stimulate environmental programmes that would not otherwise find support within the UN system. UNEP is the 'environmental conscience' of the UN system and, as such, the object of constant accusations that it is interfering in the affairs of other, more powerful, agencies (Earthscan 1982: 49).

It is impossible to avoid the paradox that, as concerted multilateral action to protect the environment becomes more urgent, it also becomes more unlikely. The reasons for this can be appreciated if we consider the concept of 'national sovereignty', which agencies like UNEP have to accommodate to. It is increasingly clear that countries are capable of enlightened conservation policies within their own national territories, while contributing to environmental degradation outside these frontiers. Japan, for example, locks away its own hardwood forests, reducing annual removals by half over a twenty year period. At the same time it takes advantage of abundant supplies of hardwoods in nearby South-East Asia 'and, now that South-East Asia's forests look likely to be depleted to commercial exhaustion by the end of the century, Japan is looking further afield, to Central America, Amazonia and West Africa' (Myers and Myers 1982: 199). Japan's attitude to conservation is not governed by environmental conviction, but by the proximity of other, poorer, countries where natural resources need to be exchanged for short-term commercial benefits. It is the global economy which underpins Japan's conservation policies, not political conviction.

In similar fashion, national governments invoke the concept of 'sovereignty' over defence policies, in quite a different way from that of economic or trade policy. During the recent conflict with Argentina the British government sought to counter demands for an international force of occupation in the Falkland Islands, partly on the grounds that the Islands were sovereign British territory. Most of the Islands were owned, of course, by a transnational company, the Falklands Island Company, and only assumed *strategic* importance for Britain on the outbreak of conflict in the South Atlantic. The notion of 'national sovereignty' is as flexible as nation-states wish it to be. The plunder of Brazil's Amazon by transnational forestry and cattle-ranching interests does not lead the Brazilian government to a defence of its sovereignty. The suggestion that international conservationists should advise Brazil how to protect these Amazonian resources does. 'Sovereignty' is invoked when questions of national 'security' are at stake, and quietly ignored when there is an international interest in the 'security' of natural resources.

It is clear that the environmental/development discourse needs to be redirected. Such a discourse acquires increased urgency in the face of a world recession. As we saw in Chapter 3 the integration of environmental assessment into the management practices of industrial society provides no guarantee that the environmental crisis will be averted. At the same time, by representing these elements in the reappraisal of capitalism which Marxism has neglected, the ecological movement has assured itself of a continuing and subversive role. Environmental management, if it means anything in the South, suggests that man is capable of inflicting on nature what he has already inflicted on himself. It does not mean that he is capable of meeting supranational threats to his resource base with supranational political action.

The way forward may be to re-examine what we mean by the 'inner limits' – the social and political imperatives behind environmental action. We have already seen how the 'outer limits', represented by the earth's resources, can be modified by technological changes, such as those promised by the new biotechnologies. The 'inner limits', our capacity to meet basic human needs for all the world's people are deter-mined by the economic and social systems under which we live. Without changing these systems radically the 'inner limits' will continue to press on resources in ways which are more harmful to some groups than to others. Conservation will continue to be seen as a management exercise, designed to ensure that a privileged population has access to a privileged environment.

Redefining the 'inner limits' imposed by human activity on the environment means recognizing that the removal of structural obstacles to development will do more to help poor people in the South than adopting notions of 'conservation' from northern industrial countries. As we have seen, in Chapters 4 and 5, poor people impose excessive strains on the carrying capacity of the natural environment because of the structural demands imposed on them. The need to increase cash income, repay debts and meet the necessities of the household impinge upon poor people while they are held in a vice by the terms of trade which govern intersectoral and international relations. As 'development' removes them from control over their own environment, this control is assumed by transnational companies and capital-intensive technologies. As some activities, especially those of women, are transferred from the household to the market place, the environment is relocated not as a part of a *local* system of production, but as a link in the international division of labour. By removing structural constraints on the activities of the poor, and imposing them on the activities of the rich, the door is opened to a more sustainable development.

The key to redirecting the development and environment discourses lies in the political and economic support given the powerless and the poor. It is an illusion to believe that environmental objectives are other than political, or other than redistributive. It is also clear that 'no new liberties can be granted from above, by institutionalised power, unless they have already been taken and put into practice by people themselves' (Gorz 1982: 11). The challenge then, is not to seek to protect the natural environment from man, but to alter the global economy in which our appetites press on the 'outer limits' of resources. This can only be done by altering the entitlements of the poor in the South so that the environmental discourse becomes a development discourse. It is possible that, entrusted with the continuation of the species, we should take our cues from societies whose very existence 'development' has always threatened.

Bibliography

Ahmed, N. U. (1975) *Field Report on Irrigation by Handpump Tubewells*, Dacca, USAID.

Alavi, H. (1982) 'The Structure of Peripheral Capitalism', in Alavi, H. and Shanin, T. (eds) *Introduction to the Sociology of Developing Societies*, London, Macmillan.

Amin, S. (1974) *Accumulation on a World Scale*, New York, Monthly Review Press.

Apthorpe, R. (1973) 'Peasants and Planistrators in Eastern Africa 1960–1970', Paper to the Association of Social Anthropologists, Oxford.

Arad, R. W. (1979) *Sharing Global Resources*, New York, McGraw-Hill.

Archetti, E. (1977) 'Analisis regional y estructura agraria en América Latina', Paper presented to seminar at El Colegio de México, unpublished manuscript.

Arizpe, L. and Arandes, T. (1981) 'The "Comparative Advantages" of Women's Disadvantages: women workers in the strawberry export agribusiness in Mexico', *Signs*, 7 (2).

Arrighi, G. and Saul, J. S. (1968) 'Socialism and Economic Development in Tropical Africa', *Journal of Modern African Studies*, 6 (2), 141–69.

Arrow, K. T. (1976) 'The Rate of Discount for Long-Term Public Investment', in Holt, A. *Energy and the Environment: a risk benefit approach*, New York, Pergamon.

Avery, D., Schramm, G. and Shapiro, K. (1978) 'Production Systems in Fragile Environments', in *Science and Technology for Managing Environments in Developing Nations*, University of Michigan.

Bahro, R. (1978) *The Alternative in Eastern Europe*, London, New Left Books.

Bahro, R. (1982a) *Socialism and Survival*, London, Heretic Books.

Bahro, R. (1982b) 'Capitalism's Global Crisis', *New Statesman*, 17 Dec.

Banaji, J. (1977) 'Modes of Production in a Materialist Conception of History', *Capital and Class*, 3.

Barbira-Scazzochio, F. (ed) (1980) *Land, People and Planning in Contemporary Amazonia*, Cambridge Centre of Latin American Studies, University of Cambridge Occasional Publication No. 3.

Barkin, D. (1978) *Desarollo regional y reorganización campesina*, Mexico City, Nueva Imagen.

Barkin, D. (1981) *The Use of Agricultural Land in Mexico*, Working Papers in US–Mexican Studies no. 17, San Diego, University of California.

Barnes, B. and Edge, D. (eds) (1982) *Science in Context: readings in the sociology of science*, Milton Keynes, Open University Press.

Barraclough, S. (1973) *Agrarian Structure in Latin America*, Massachusetts, D. C. Heath.

Barraclough, S. and Domike, A. (1970) 'Agrarian Structure in Seven Latin American Countries', in *Agrarian Problems and Peasant Movements in Latin America*, New York, Anchor Doubleday.

Bartra, A. (1976) 'Colectivización o proletarización: el caso del Plan Chontalpa', *Cuadernos Agrarios*, 1 (4).

Bartra, R. (1974) *Estructura agraria y clases sociales en México*, Mexico City, Serie Popular Era.

Barzelay, M. and Pearson, S. R. (1982) 'The Efficiency of Producing Alcohol for Energy in Brazil', *Economic Development and Cultural Change*, 31 (1).

Bauer, P. T. (1981) *Equality, the Third World and Economic Delusion*, London, Methuen.

Bauer, P. T. and Yamey, B. S. (1957) *The Economics of Underdeveloped Countries*, Cambridge, Cambridge University Press.

Bell, C. (1974) 'Ideology and Economic Interests in Indian Land Reform', in Lehmann, D. (ed.) *Agrarian Reform and Agrarian Reformism*, London, Faber.

Bergmann, T. (1977) *The Development Models of India, the Soviet Union and China*, Assen, Van Gorcum.

Bernstein, H. (ed.) (1973) *Underdevelopment and Development*, Harmondsworth, Penguin.

Bernstein, H. (1977) 'Notes on Capital and Peasantry', *Review of African Political Economy*, 10, 60–73.

Bernstein, H. (1979) 'African Peasantries: a theoretical framework', *The Journal of Peasant Studies*, 6 (4).

Beteille, A. (1974) *Studies in Agrarian Social Structure*, Oxford, Oxford University Press.

Biggs, S. (1981) 'Monitoring for Re-planning Purposes: the role of research and development in river basin development', in Saha, S. K. and Barrow, C. (eds) *River Basin Planning: theory and practice*, Chichester, John Wiley.

Biggs, S. D. and Burns, C. E. (1976) 'Transactions, modes and the distribution of farm output', in Joy, J. L. (ed.) *The Kosi Symposium: the Rural Problem in N. E. Bihar*, Brighton, Institute of Development Studies.

Biggs, S. D. and Clay, E. J. (1981) 'Sources of Innovation in Agricultural Technology', *World Development*, 9 (4).

Biswas, M. R. and Biswas, A. K. (1978) 'Loss of Productive Soil', in *International Journal of Environmental Studies*, 12.

Blaikie, P. (1981) 'Class, Land-Use and Soil Erosion', Paper read to the Development Studies Association Annual Conference, Oxford.

Bookchin, M. (1980) *Towards an Ecological Society*, Montreal, Black Rose Books.

Booth, D. (1975) 'Andre Gunder Frank: an introduction and appreciation', in Oxaal, I., Barnett, T. and Booth, D. (eds) *Beyond the Sociology of Development*, London, Routledge & Kegan Paul.

Boserup, E. (1981) *Population and Technology*, Oxford, Basil Blackwell.

Bottomore, T. (1982) 'Degrees of Determination', *The Times Literary Supplement*, London, 12 March.

Bowonder, B. (1981) 'The Myth and Reality of High Yielding Varieties in Indian Agriculture', *Development and Change*, 12 (2).

Bradby, B. (1975) 'The Destruction of Natural Economy', *Economy and Society*, 4 (2).

Brading, D. (1978) *Haciendas and Ranchos in the Mexican Bajio*, Cambridge, Cambridge University Press.

Brandt Commission (1980) *North-South: a programme for survival*, London, Pan Books.

Brandt Commission (1983) *Common Crisis*, London, Pan Books.

Bromley, R. and Gerry, C. (1979) *Casual Work and Poverty in Third World Cities*, Chichester, John Wiley.

Brookfield, H. (1975) *Interdependent Development*, London, Methuen.

Brookfield, H. (1982) 'On Man and Ecosystems', *International Social Science Journal*, xxxiv (3).

Brooks, H. (1976) 'Environmental Decision Making: analysis and values', in Tribe, L. H., Schelling, C. S. and Voss, I. (eds) *When Values Conflict: essays on environmental analysis, discourse and decision*, Cambridge, Mass., Ballinger.

Brown, L. R. (1978) *The Twenty-Ninth Day*, New York, Norton.

Bull, D. (1982) *A Growing Problem: pesticides and the Third World poor*, Oxford, OXFAM.

Burbach, R. and Flynn, P. (1980) *Agribusiness in the Americas*, New York, Monthly Review Press.

Buttel, F. (1979) 'Agricultural Structure and Energy Intensity: a comparative analysis of the developed capitalist societies', Comparative

Rural and Regional Studies, University of Guelph, Occasional Paper No. 1.

Byres, T. (1974) 'Land Reform, Industrialization and the Marketed Surplus in India: an essay on the power of rural bias', in Lehmann, D. (ed.) *Agrarian Reform and Agrarian Reformism*, London, Faber.

Byres, T. (1977) 'Agrarian transition and the agrarian question', *Journal of Peasant Studies*, 4 (3).

Byres, T. (1979) 'Of Neo-Populist Pipe-Dreams: Daedalus in the Third World and the myth of urban bias', *Journal of Peasant Studies*, 6 (2), 210–44.

Caldwell, M. (1977) *The Wealth of Some Nations*, London, Zed Press.

Capra, F. (1981) 'The Yin Yang Balance', *Resurgence*, 86.

Cardoso, F. H. (1972) 'Dependent Capitalist Development in Latin America' *New Left Review*, 74.

Cardoso, F. H. (1980) 'Development and Environment: the Brazilian case', *CEPAL Review*, 12.

Castells, M. (1977) *The Urban Question: a Marxist approach*, London, Edward Arnold.

Castillo, L. and Lehmann, D. (1982) 'Chile's Three Agrarian Reforms: the inheritors', *Bulletin of Latin American Research*, 1 (2).

Chambers, R. (1977) 'Notes and Comments: technology and peasant production', *Development and Change* 8, 347–75.

Chambers, R. (1981) 'Introduction' to Chambers, R., Longhurst, R. and Pacey, A. (eds) *Seasonal Dimensions to Rural Poverty*, London, Frances Pinter.

Chowdury, A. K. M. A., Huffman, S. L. and Chen, L. C. (1981) 'Agriculture and Nutrition in Matlab Thana, Bangladesh', in Chambers, R., Longhurst, R. and Pacey, A. (eds) *Seasonal Dimensions to Rural Poverty*, London, Frances Pinter.

CIMMYT (The International Centre for the Improvement of Maize and Wheat) (1974) *The Puebla Project – Seven Years of Experience 1966–1973*, Mexico City.

Clark, C. and Haswell, M. (1964) *The Economics of Subsistence Agriculture*, London, Macmillan.

Clay, E. J. (1980) 'The Economics of Bamboo Tubewell' *Ceres*, 13 (3) 43–7.

Clay, E. J. (1981) 'Seasonal Patterns of Agricultural Employment in Bangladesh', in Chambers, R., Longhurst, R. and Pacey, A. (eds) *Seasonal Dimensions to Rural Poverty*, London, Frances Pinter.

Cliffe, L. (1982) 'Class Formation as an "Articulation" Process: East African cases', in Alavi, H. and Shanin, T. (eds) *Introduction to the Sociology of Developing Societies*, London, Macmillan.

Clutterbuck, C. and Lang, T. (1982) *More Than We Can Chew: the crazy world of food and farming*, London, Pluto Press.

Collinson, M. (1979) 'Micro-level Accomplishment and Challenges for the Less Developed World', Paper to International Association of Agricultural Economists, 17th Conference, Canada, Banff.

Commoner, B. (1972) *The Closing Circle*, London, Jonathan Cape.

Cotgrove, S. (1983) 'Environmentalism and Utopia', in O'Riordan, T. and Turner, R. Kerry (eds) *An Annotated Reader in Environmental Planning and Management*, Oxford, Pergamon.

Cuanalo, M. (1983) *Social and Economic Constraints to Firewood Production in Mexico: a preliminary report*, London, Overseas Development Administration.

Dasmann, R. F. (1975) *The Conservation Alternative*, Chichester, John Wiley.

Delavaud, A. C. (1980) 'From Colonization to Agricultural Development: the case of coastal Ecuador', in Preston, D. (ed.) *Environment, Society and Rural Change in Latin America*, Chichester, John Wiley.

Descartes, R. (1968) *Discours de la méthode*, Paris, Larousse.

Dickson, D. (1974) *Alternative Technology*, London, Fontana.

D'Incao e Mello, M. C. (1976) *O 'Boia-Fria': acumulacao e miseria*, Petropolis, Brazil, Editôria Vozes.

Dinham, B. and Hines, C. (1983) *Agribusiness in Africa*, London, Earth Resources.

Earthscan (1982) *Stockholm Plus Ten*, Earthscan Press Briefing Document, no. 31.

Ebert, F. Foundation (1981) *Towards One World? International Responses to the Brandt Report*, London, Temple Smith.

Eckholm, E. P. (1976) *Losing Ground: environmental stress and world food prospects*, Oxford, Pergamon.

Eckholm, E. P. (1982) *Down to Earth: environment and human needs*, London, Pluto Press.

Eckstein, S. (1977) *The Poverty of Revolution, the State and the Urban Poor in Mexico*, Princeton, Princeton University Press.

Elliott, C. (1982) 'Making Excellence Useful', Conference on 'Technical Assistance Overseas and the Environment', London, Royal Society of Arts.

Emmanuel, A. (1973) *Unequal Exchange*, London, New Left Books.

Emmanuel, A. (1982) *Appropriate or Underdeveloped Technology?*, Chichester, John Wiley.

Engels, F. (1970a) 'Introduction to the Dialectics of Nature', in Marx, K. and Engels, F. *Selected Works* (one volume), London, Lawrence & Wishart.

Engels, F. (1970b) 'The Part played by Labour in the Transition from Ape to Man', in Marx, K. and Engels, F. *Selected Works* (one volume), London, Lawrence & Wishart.

Engels, F. (1970c) 'The Origins of the Family, Private Property and the State', in Marx, K. and Engels, F. *Selected Works* (one volume), London, Lawrence & Wishart.

Environmental Conservation (1982) 9 (2).

Erasmus, C. (1968) 'Community Development and the Emcogido Syndrome', *Human Organization*, 27 (1), Spring.

Esteva, G. (1975) 'La agricultura en México de 1950 a 1979: el fracaso de una falsa analogía', *Comercio Exterior*, 25 (12).

Esteva, G. (1980) 'La experiencia de la intervención estatal reguladora en la comercialización agropecuaria de 1970 a 1976', in Oswald, U. (ed.) *Mercado y Dependencia*, Mexico, Nueva Imagen.

Evans, D. D. and Adler, L. N. (eds) (1979) *Appropriate Technology for Development: a discussion and case histories*, Boulder, Westview Press.

Ewell, P. T. and Poleman, T. T. (1980) *Uxpanapa: agricultural development in the Mexican tropics*, Oxford, Pergamon.

Farmer, B. H. (1977) *Green Revolution? technology and change in rice-growing areas of Tamil Nadu and Sri Lanka*, London, Macmillan.

Fernandez, Luis M. (1979) 'Ganaderia, campesinado y productos de granos basicos: un estudio en chiapas', Mexico City, Fundación Javier Bamos Sierra.

Food and Agricultural Organisation (FAO) (1978) *The State of Food and Agriculture 1977*, Rome.

Foster, G. M. (1965) 'Peasant society and the image of limited good', *American Anthropologist*, 67 (2), 293–315.

Foster-Carter, A. (1974) 'Neo-Marxist Approaches to Development and Underdevelopment', in de Kadt, E. and Williams, G. (eds) *Sociology and Development*, London, Tavistock.

Frank, A. G. (1967) *Capitalism and Underdevelopment in Latin America*, New York, Monthly Review Press.

Frank, A. G. (1969) *Latin America: underdevelopment or revolution*, New York, Monthly Review Press.

Fraser Darling (1970) *Wilderness and Plenty* (1969 Reith Lectures), London, BBC Publications.

Furtado, C. (1970) *Economic Development of Latin America*, Cambridge, Cambridge University Press.

Fromm, E. (1979) *To have or to be?*, London, Sphere Books.

Galjart, B. (1979) 'Peasant cooperation, consciousness and solidarity', *Development and Change*, VI (4).

Gamser, M. S. (1980) 'The Forest Resource and Rural Energy Development', *World Development*, 8.

Geertz, C. (1971) *Agricultural Involution*, Berkeley, University of California Press.

Gerth, H. H. and Wright Mills, C. (1970) *From Max Weber: essays in sociology*, London, Routledge & Kegan Paul.

Global 2000 (1982) *Report to the President*, Harmondsworth, Penguin.

Godelier, M. (1977) *Perspectives in Marxist Anthropology*, Cambridge, Cambridge University Press.

Goodman, D. and Redclift, M. (1981) *From Peasant to Proletarian: capitalist development and agrarian transitions*, Oxford, Basil Blackwell.

Gorz, A. (1982) *Farewell to the Working Class: an essay on post-industrial socialism*, London, Pluto Press.

Gostyla, L. and Whyte, W. F. (1979) 'ICTA in Guatema', Centre for International Studies, Cornell University, unpublished manuscript.

Griffin, K. (1969) *Underdevelopment in Spanish America: an interpretation*, London, Allen & Unwin.

Griffin, K. (1974) *The Political Economy of Agrarian Change*, London, Macmillan.

Griffin, K. (1976) *Land Distribution and Rural Poverty*, London, Macmillan.

Griffin, S. (1980) *Woman and Nature: the roaring inside her*, New York, Harper Colophon Books.

Grindle, M. (1977) *Bureaucrats, Politicians and Peasants in Mexico*, Berkeley, University of California Press.

Guillet, D. (1979) *Agrarian Reform and Peasant Economy in Southern Peru*, Columbia, University of Missouri Press.

Gutelman, M. (1974) *Capitalismo y Reforma Agraria en México*, Mexico City, Ediciones Era.

Gutkind, P. C. and Waterman, P. (1977) *African Social Studies: a radical reader*, London, Heinemann.

Habermas, J. (1976) 'Systematically Distorted Communication', in Connerton, P. (ed.) *Critical Sociology: selected readings*, Harmondsworth, Penguin.

Harriss, J. (1981) *Capitalist and Peasant Farming*, Bombay, Oxford University Press.

Hewitt, C. (1976) *Modernizing Mexican Agriculture*, Geneva, UNRISD.

Heyer, J., Roberts, P. and Williams, G. (eds) (1981) *Rural Development in Tropical Africa*, London, Macmillan.

Hirsch, F. (1977) *The Social Limits to Growth*, London, Routledge & Kegan Paul.

Hobsbawm, E. (1969) 'A Case of Neo-Feudalism: la Convención, Peru' *Journal of Latin American Studies*, 1 (1).

Hodder, B. W. (1968) *Economic Development in the Tropics*, London Methuen.

Huizer, G. (1970) *Human Organization*, 23 (4).

Hutton, C. and Cohen, R. (1975) 'African Peasants and Resistance t Change: a reconsideration of sociological approaches', in Oxaal, I. Barnett, T. and Booth, D. (eds) *Beyond the Sociology of Development* London, Routledge & Kegan Paul.

IBRD International Bank for Reconstruction and Development (1979 Measuring Project Impact: PIDER Rural Development Project World Bank Staff Working Paper, No. 332, Washington DC.

IBRD (1983) *Community Participation in Local Investment Programming: a social methodology in PIDER-Mexico*, draft working paper, Washington, DC.

ICRISAT (International Crops Research Institute for the Semi-arid Tropics) (1980) Proceedings of the International Workshop on socio-economic constraints to development of semi-arid tropical agriculture, Hyderabad.

IDRC (International Development Research Centre) (1982) *Agricultural Policy in India*, Ottawa.

ILO (International Labour Office) (1977) *Poverty and Landlessness in Rural Asia*, Geneva.

IPPF (International Planned Parenthood Federation) (1982) 'Bangladesh: a fragile but too fertile delta', *People*, 9 (2).

de Janvry, A. (1981) *The Agrarian Question and Reformism in Latin America*, Baltimore, Maryland, John Hopkins University Press.

Jeffery, S. (1981) '"Our Usual Landslide": ubiquitous hazard and socio-economic causes of natural disaster in Nusa Teuggara Timur, Indonesia', in Natural Hazards Research Working Paper, No. 40, Boulder, University of Colorado.

Jodha, N. S. (1979) *Intercropping in traditional Farming Systems*, ICRISAT.

Jones, A. (1983) 'Beyond Industrial Society: towards balance and harmony in an eco-future', paper delivered to the British Sociological Association Annual Conference.

Jones, E. L. and Woolf, S. J. (1969) *Agrarian Change and Economic Development*, London, Methuen.

Kelly, P. F. (1980) 'Mexican Border Industrialisation, Female Labour Force Participation and Industrialisation', *Signs*, mimeo.

Khan, A. R. (1977) 'Poverty and Inequality in Rural Bangladesh', in

Poverty and Landlessness in Rural Asia, International Labour Office, Geneva.

Khozin, G. (1979) *The Biosphere and Politics*, Moscow, Progress Publishers.

King, A. (1980) *The State of the Planet*, Oxford, Pergamon.

King, Y. (1981) 'Feminism and the Revolt of Nature', *Heresies* 13, 4 (1).

Kirpich, P. Z. (1979) 'El desarrollo de las planices tropicales en América Latina', *Comercio Exterior*, 29 (9).

Kitching, G. (1980) *Class and Economic Change in Kenya: the making of an African petite-bourgeoisie 1905–1970*, New Haven, Yale University Press.

Kitching, G. (1982) *Development and Underdevelopment in Historical Perspective*, London, Methuen.

Kumar, K. (1978) *Prophecy and Progress*, Harmondsworth, Penguin.

Laclau, E. (1971) 'Feudalism and Capitalism in Latin America', *New Left Review*, 67.

Lappé, F. M. and Collins, J. (1977) *Food First: beyond the myth of scarcity*, New York, Houghton Mifflin.

Lappé, F. M. and Collins, J. (1978) *World Hunger: ten myths*, San Francisco, Institute for Food and Development Policy.

Leach, G. (1976) *Energy and Food Production*, Guildford, IPC.

Lehmann, D. (1978) 'The Death of Land Reform: a polemic', *World Development*, 6 (3).

Lehmann, D. (1982) 'Agrarian Structure, Migration and the State in Cuba', in Peek, P. and Standing, G. (eds) *State Policies and Migration*, London, Croom Helm.

Leland, S. (1981) 'The Earth Without Violence', *Resurgence*, 86.

Lenin, V. I. (1952) *Materialism and Empirio-Criticism*, Moscow, Progress Publishers.

Lenin, V. I. (1964) *The Development of Capitalism in Russia (Collected Works*, vol. 3), Moscow, Progress Publishers.

Lenin, V. I. (1972) *Imperialism, The Highest Stage of Capitalism*, Moscow, Progress Publishers.

Leowontin, S. (1979) 'The Green Revolution and Capitalist Development in Mexico since 1940', Paper presented to the Symposium, 'Food, Ecology, Culture, Economy and Nutrition', Yale University.

Lewis, W. A. (1955) *The Theory of Economic Growth*, London, Allen & Unwin.

Leys, C. (1977) *Underdevelopment in Kenya: the political economy of neo-colonialism 1964–1971*, London, Heinemann.

Lipton, M. (1977) *Why Poor People Stay Poor: a study of urban bias in world development*, London, Temple Smith.

Lipton, M. (1978) 'Inter-Farm, Inter-Regional and Farm-Non-Farm

Income Distribution: the impact of new cereal varieties', *World Development*, 6 (3).

Lofchie, M. F. (1975) 'Political and Economic Origins of African Hunger', *Journal of Modern African Studies*, 14.

Lomnitz, L. (1982) 'Horizontal and Vertical Relations and the Social Structure of Urban Mexico', *Latin American Research Review*, XVII (2).

Long, N. (1977) *An Introduction to the Sociology of Rural Development*, London, Tavistock.

Long, N. and Roberts, B. (eds) (1979) *Peasant Cooperation and Capitalist Farming in Central Peru*, University of Texas.

Longman, K. A. and Jenik, J. (1974) *Tropical Forest and its Environment*, Harlow, Longman.

Lopes, B. J. R. (1978) 'Capitalist Development and Agrarian Structure in Brazil', *International Journal of Urban and Regional Research* 2 (1).

Lowe, P. and Goyder, J. (1983) *Environmental Groups in Politics*, London, Allen & Unwin.

Lowe, P. and Worboys, M. (1980) 'Ecology and Ideology', in Buttel, F. H. and Newby, H. (eds) *The Rural Sociology of the Advanced Societies*, London, Croom Helm.

Luiselli, C. (1979) 'Agricultura y alimentación en México: premisas para una nueva estrategia', *Estudios Rurales Latinoamericanos*, 2 (3).

Luxemburg, R. (1951) *The Accumulation of Capital*, London, Routledge & Kegan Paul.

McClelland (1961) *The Achieving Society*, Glencoe, Illinois, Free Press.

Magdoff, H. (1982) 'Imperialism: a historical survey', in Alavi, H. and Shanin, T. (eds) *Introduction to the Sociology of Developing Societies*, London, Macmillan.

Marnham, P. (1977) *Nomads of the Sahel*, London, Minority Rights Group.

Martinez Alier, J. (1977) *Haciendas, Plantations and Collective Farms: agrarian class societies*, London, Frank Cass.

Marx, K. (1974) *Capital*, vol. 3, Moscow, Progress Publishers.

Marx, K. and Engels, F. (1970) *Selected Works* (one volume), London, Lawrence & Wishart.

Maxwell, S. (1983) 'Farming Systems Research: a course of lectures', mimeo (unpublished).

Meadows, D. C., Randers, D. H. and Behrens, W. W. (1972) *The Limits to Growth*, London, Pan Books.

Meijer, W. (1980) 'A New Look at the Plight of Tropical Rain-Forests', *Environmental Conservation*, 7 (3).

Meissner, F. (1981) 'The Mexican Food System (SAM): cultivating the oil revenue', *Food Policy*, 6 (4).

Merchant, C. (1980) *The Death of Nature: women, ecology and the scientific revolution*, New York, Harper & Row.

Mill, J. S. (1873) *Principles of Political Economy*, London.

Mitchell, S. (ed.) (1981) *The Logic of Poverty: the case of the Brazilian Northeast*, London, Routledge & Kegan Paul.

Monzelis, N. (1976) 'Capitalism and the Development of Agriculture', *Journal of Peasant Studies*, 3 (4).

Mooney, P. R. (1979) *Seeds of the Earth*, Washington, DC, ICDA.

Moore, M. and Harriss, J. (1984) (eds) 'Development and the Rural-Urban Divider', *Journal of Development Studies*, Special Number (forthcoming).

Moran, E. F. (1982) 'Ecological, Anthropological and Agronomic Research in the Amazon Basin', *Latin American Research Review*, XVII (1).

Mujica, R. (1978) 'Las zonas de riego: acumulacion y marginalidad', *Comercio Exterior*, 29 (4).

Myers, N. (1979) *The Sinking Ark*, Oxford, Pergamon.

Myers, N. and Myers, D. (1982) 'Increasing Awareness of the Supranational Nature of Emerging Environmental Issues', *Ambio* XI (4).

Nelson, N. (1979) *Why Has Development Neglected Rural Women?*, Oxford, Pergamon.

Newby, H. (1980a) 'Rural Sociology: a trend report', *Current Sociology*, 28 (1).

Newby, H. (1980b) *Green and Pleasant Land*, Harmondsworth, Penguin.

Newby, H., Rose, D. and Saunders, P. (1978) *Property, Paternalism and Power: class and control in rural England*, London, Hutchinson.

Norman, D. W. (1972) 'Farming Systems Research to Improve Livelihood of Small Farmers', *American Journal of Agricultural Economics*, 60 (5).

Norton, B. E. (1976) 'The Management of Desert Grazing Systems', in Glantz, M. H. (ed.) *The Politics of Natural Disaster: the case of the Sahel drought*, New York, Praeger.

Norton-Taylor, R. (1982) *Whose Land Is It Anyway?*, Wellingborough, Northamptonshire, Turnstone Press.

de Oliveira, F. (1981) 'State and Society in Northeastern Brazil: SUDENE and the role of regional planning', in Mitchell, S. (ed.) *The Logic of Poverty: the case of the Brazilian Northeast*, London, Routledge & Kegan Paul.

O'Riordan, T. (1981) *Environmentalism*, London, Pion.

O'Riordan, T. and Turner, R. Kerry (1983) *An Annotated Reader in Environmental Planning and Management*, Oxford, Pergamon.

Oxaal, I., Barnett, T. and Booth, D. (eds) (1975) *Beyond the Sociology of Development*, London, Routledge & Kegan Paul.

Paré, L. (1977) *El proletariado agricola en Mexico*, Mexico City, Siglo XXI.

Pearse, A. (1974) *The Social and Economic Implications of the Large-Scale Introduction of High-Yielding Varieties of Foodgrain*, Geneva, UNRISD.

Pearse, A. (1980) *Seeds of Plenty, Seeds of Change*, Oxford, Clarendon Press.

Perlman, J. (1976) *The Myth of Marginality*, Berkeley, University of California Press.

Pickvance, C. (ed.) (1976) *Urban Sociology: critical essays*, London, Methuen.

Plumwood, V. and Routley, R. (1982) 'World Rain Forest Destruction: the social factors', *The Ecologist*, 12 (1).

Posner, J. L. and McPherson, M. F. (1981) 'The Steep Sloped Areas of Tropical America: current situation and prospects for the year 2000', New York, Rockefeller Foundation, Agricultural Sciences Division.

Preston, D. (ed.) (1980) *Environment, Society and Rural Change in Latin America*, Chichester, John Wiley.

Preston, D. and Redclift, M. R. (1980) 'Agrarian Reform and Rural Change in Ecuador' in Preston, D. (ed.) *Environment, Society and Rural Change in Latin America*, Chichester, John Wiley.

Rada, J. F. (1981) 'The Microelectronics Revolution: implications for the Third World', *Development Dialogue*, 2.

Rainbird, H. (1981) *Peasant Structure and Agrarian Reform in Highland Peru*, University of Durham, Ph.D. thesis.

Redclift, M. (1980) 'Agrarian Populism in Mexico – the "via campesina"', *Journal of Peasant Studies*, 7 (4).

Redclift, M. (1981a) 'The Mexican Food System (SAM): sowing subsidies, reaping apathy', *Food Policy*, 6 (4).

Redclift, M. (1981b) 'Development Policymaking in Mexico: *the Sistema Alimentario Mexicano*', Working Paper in US–Mexican Studies, No. 24, San Diego, University of California.

Redclift, M. (1983) 'Production Programs for Small Farmers: Plan Puebla as myth and reality', *Economic Development and Cultural Change*, 31 (3).

Redclift, N. (1982) 'Relations of Gender and the International Division of Labour', paper delivered to meeting of the International Sociological Association, Mexico City.

Redclift, N. and Mingione, E. (eds) (1984) *Beyond Employment, Household, Gender and Subsistence*, Oxford, Basil Blackwell.

Revel-Mouroz, T. (1980) 'Mexican Colonization Experience in the

Humid Tropics', in Preston, D. (ed.) *Environment, Society and Rural Change in Latin America*, Chichester, John Wiley.

Review of Economic Situation of Mexico (1979) Banco Nacional de Mexico, 54 (637).

Riddell, R. (1981) *Ecodevelopment*, Farnborough, Gower.

Roberts, B. (1978) *Cities of Peasants*, London, Edward Arnold.

Rogers, B. (1981) *The Domestication of Women*, London, Tavistock.

Roxborough, I. (1979) *Theories of Underdevelopment*, London, Macmillan.

Runciman, W. G. (1966) *Relative Deprivation and Social Justice*, London, Routledge & Kegan Paul.

Rusque, J. (1982) *Labour Absorption and the Persistence of the Peasant Sector: a case study in Cañar Province, Highland Ecuador*, Swansea, University College of Wales, Ph.D. thesis.

Rutsch, M. (1980) *La Cuestion Ganadera en Mexico*, Mexico City, CIIS.

Saint, W. (1982) 'Farming for Energy: social options under Brazil's National Alcohol Programme', *World Development*, 10 (3).

Sandbach, F. (1980) *Environment, Ideology and Policy*, Oxford, Basil Blackwell.

Sandbrook, R. (1982) 'What the UK Should and Could Do', Conference on 'Technical Assistance Overseas and the Environment', London, Royal Society of Arts.

Saul, J. S. and Woods, R. (1971) 'African Peasantries', in Shanin, T. (ed.) *Peasants and Peasant Societies*, Harmondsworth, Penguin.

Schryer, F. (1980) *The Rancheros of Pisaflores*, Toronto, University of Toronto Press.

Schumacher, E. F. (1973) *Small is Beautiful*, New York, Harper & Row.

Scott, C. (1976) 'Peasants, Proletarianisation and the Articulation of Modes of Production: the case of sugar-cane cutters in Northern Peru, 1940–1969', *Journal of Peasant Studies*, 3 (3).

Sen, A. (1981) *Poverty and Famines: an essay on entitlement and deprivation*, Oxford, Oxford University Press.

Sheets, H. and Morris, R. (1976) 'Disaster in the Desert', in Glantz, M. H. (ed.) *The Politics of Natural Disaster: the case of the Sahel drought*, New York, Praeger.

Shepherd, A. (1981) 'Capitalist Agriculture in Africa', paper presented to the IVth Bi-Annual Conference of the African Association of Political Science, Harare, Zimbabwe.

Shepherd, A. (1982) 'Agricultural Capitalism and Rural Development in the Sudan', paper presented to the Development Studies Association, Dublin.

de Silva, S. B. D. (1982) *The Political Economy of Underdevelopment*, London, Routledge & Kegan Paul.

Simmie, J. (1974) *Citizens in Conflict: the sociology of town planning*, London, Hutchinson.

Simmons, I. (1974) *The Ecology of Natural Resources*, London, Edward Arnold.

Sinha, R. (1977) 'The World Food Problem: consensus and conflict', *World Development*, 5 (5–7).

Skolimowski, H. (1981) *Eco-Philosophy*, London, Marion Boyars.

Smith, J. E. (1981) *Biotechnology*, London, Edward Arnold.

Socolow, R. H. (1976) 'Failures of Discourse: obstacles to the integration of environmental values into Natural Resource policy', in Tribe, L. H., Schelling, C. S. and Voss, I. (eds) *When Values Conflict: essays on environmental analysis, discourse and decision*, Cambridge, Mass., Ballinger.

Stewart, F. (1977) *Technology and Underdevelopment*, London, Macmillan.

Stewart, F. (1983) 'Appropriate or Underdeveloped Technology?' (Book Review of Emmanuel) *Appropriate Technology*, 9 (4).

Stretton, H. (1976) *Capitalism, Socialism and the Environment*, Cambridge, Cambridge University Press.

Sunkel, O. (1980) 'The Interaction between Styles of Development and the Environment in Latin America', *CEPAL Review*, 12.

Sutcliffe, B. (1983) *Hard Times: the world economy in turmoil*, London, Pluto Press.

Tarris, M. (1976) 'Environmental Values', in Tribe, L. H., Schelling, C. S. and Voss, I. (eds) *When Values Conflict: essays on environmental analysis, discourse and decision*, Cambridge, Mass., Ballinger.

Taylor, B. (1983) *Eve and the New Jerusalem: socialism and feminism in the nineteenth century*, London, Virago.

Thomas, K. (1983) *Man and the Natural World: changing attitudes in England 1500–1800*, London, Allen Lane.

Townsend, P. (1971) *The Concept of Poverty*, London, Heinemann.

Townsend, P. (1974) 'Poverty as Relative Deprivation: resources and styles of living', in Wedderburn, D. (ed.) *Poverty, Inequality and Class Structure*, Cambridge, Cambridge University Press.

Tribe, L. H. Schelling, C. S. and Voss, I. (eds) (1976) *When Values Conflict: essays on environmental analysis, discourse and decision*, Cambridge, Mass., Ballinger.

Trigo, E., Pineiro, M. and Fiorentino, R. (1979) 'Technical change in Latin American agriculture', *Food Policy*, 4 (3).

Turner, J. F. C. (1976) *Housing by People*, London, Marion Boyars.

Turrent, A. (1979) 'El sistema agrícola: un marco de referencia necesario para la planeación de la investigación en México', Mexico City, unpublished manuscript.

UNEP (United Nations Environment Programme) (1981) *Environment and Development in Africa*, Oxford, Pergamon.

UNESCO (1982) *International Social Science Journal*, xxxiv (3).

United Nations (1972) *Development and the Environment*, Reports and Working Papers of a panel of experts convened by the Secretary-General of the United Nations, Paris, Mouton.

Vallianatos, E. G. (1976) *Fear in the Countryside*, Cambridge, Mass., Ballinger.

Van den Bosch, R. (1980) *The Pesticide Conspiracy*, London, Prism Press.

Van der Pluijin, T. (1982) 'Energy versus Food? Implications of macro-economic adjustments on land-use patterns: the ethanol programme in Brazil', *Boletin de Estudios Latinoamericanos*, 33.

Van der Velde, J. (1980) 'Water Development' in Coward, E. Walter (ed.) *Irrigation and Agricultural Development in Asia: perspectives from the social sciences*, Ithaca, Cornell University Press.

Wade, R. (1979) 'The Social Response to Irrigation: an Indian case study', *Journal of Development Studies*, 16 (1).

Wade, R. (1982) 'The System of Administrative and Political Corruption: canal irrigation in South India', *Journal of Development Studies*, 18 (2).

Wallenstein, I. (1974) *The Modern World System: capitalist agriculture and the European world economy*, New York, Academic Press.

Ward, B. (1979) *Progress for a Small Planet*, Harmondsworth, Penguin.

Warman, A. (1976) *Y Venimos a Contradecir*, Mexico City, Ediciones Casa Chata.

Warren, B. (1973) 'Imperialism and Capitalist Industrialization', *New Left Review*, 81.

Wellhausen, E. (1976) 'The Agriculture of Mexico', *Scientific American*, 235 (3).

WHO (World Health Organization) (1976) 'Community Water Supply and Waste-water Disposal', Geneva.

Willet, J. W. (1973) 'Food Needs and Effective Demand for Food', in Poleman, T. and Freebairn, D. (eds) *Food, Population and Employment: the impact of the Green Revolution*, New York, Praeger.

Williams, G. (ed.) (1976) *Nigeria, Economy and Society*, London, Collins.

Williams, G. and Allen, C. (ed.) (1981) *Sociology of Developing Countries: Sub-Saharan Africa*, London, Macmillan.

Williams, R. (1981) 'Socialism and Ecology', London, SERA.

Winder, D. (1977) 'Land Development in Mexico: a case study', *Institute of Development Studies Bulletin*, 8 (4).

Wittfogel, K. A. (1957) *Oriental Despotism: a comparative study of total power*, New Haven, Yale University Press.

Wolfe, M. (1980) 'The Environment in the Political Arena', *CEPAL Review*, 12.

World Conservation Strategy (1980) Living Resource Conservation for Sustainable Development, International Union for Conservation of Nature and Natural Resources, Gland, Switzerland.

Worthington, E. B. (1982) 'World Campaign for the Biosphere', *Environmental Conservation*, 9 (2).

Yates, L. P. (1981) *Mexico's Agricultural Dilemma*, Tucson, University of Arizona Press.

Index